Faith Roots

SNAPSHOTS
OF THE BIG PICTURE

An ADVENT Family Devotional

Mindy Lee Hopman

D1511845

Copyright © 2018 by Mindy Lee Hopman
All Rights Reserved.

Faith Roots: An ADVENT Family Devotional

Published by B New Creations, Gulf Breeze, FL 32563
ISBN 978-0-9984648-5-5

All photographs captured by the author, Mindy Lee Hopman unless otherwise indicated. All rights reserved.

No portion of this book may be reproduced, stored in a retrieval system, or transmitted in any form or by any means—electronic, mechanical, photocopy, recording, scanning, or any other, except for brief quotations in critical reviews or articles—without the prior written permission of the publisher. The author guarantees all contents are original and do not infringe upon the legal rights of any other person or work.

Unless otherwise indicated, Bible quotations are taken from the New American Standard Bible (NASB). Copyright © 1960, 1962, 1963, 1968, 1971, 1972, 1973, 1975, 1977, 1995 by The Lockman Foundation. Used by permission. www.lockman.org. All rights reserved.

Scripture quotations marked (NIV) are taken from the Holy Bible, New International Version®, NIV®. Copyright © 1973, 1978, 1984, 2011 by Biblica, Inc.™ Used by permission of Zondervan. All rights reserved worldwide. www.zondervan.com The "NIV" and "New International Version" are trademarks registered in the United States Patent and Trademark Office by Biblica, Inc.™ Used with permission.

Scripture quotations marked (KJV) are from the New King James Version®. Copyright © 1982 by Thomas Nelson, Inc. Used by permission. All rights reserved.

Scripture quotations marked (ESV) are from The Holy Bible, English Standard Version® (ESV®), copyright© 2001 by Crossway, a publishing ministry of Good News Publishers. Used by permission. All rights reserved.

Scripture quotations marked (KJV) are from The Authorized (King James) Version. Rights in the Authorized Version in the United Kingdom are vested in the Crown. Reproduced by permission of the Crown's patentee, Cambridge University Press.

Scriptures quotations marked (NLT) are taken from the Holy Bible, New Living Translation: Copyright© 1996, 2004, 2007 by Tyndale House Foundation. Used by permission of Tyndale House Publishers, Inc., Carol Stream, Illinois 60188. All rights reserved.

3579864

To my children
Hunter and Haylee

While we await the coming of the Messiah,
the Advent season begins on the fourth Sunday before Christmas,
which normally falls between November 27th and December 3rd each year.

Advent ends on Christmas Eve, however,
Faith Roots: An Advent Family Devotional will lead you
a little past the Christmas holiday as we experience the
wonder of his love together and turn our focus to the joy
He brought to the world and the anticipation of when He will return!

TABLE OF CONTENTS

And I will *bless*
those who bless you,
And the one who
curses you I will curse.
And in you
all the families
of the earth
will be blessed.

~Genesis 12:3

INTRODUCTION

There is something special about this time of year.

A quiet stillness sits in the cool air as we wait with wonder and anticipate the celebration of the One who has come as a descendant of Abraham to bless all the families of the earth.

The King of kings came as a baby over 2,000 years ago, not born to royalty in a shiny palace, but born in a manger next to the animals' trough. Why was royalty born in such an odd place?

Because God's ways are not our ways. They are higher. In fact, His ways are often the exact opposite of our own human perspectives which leaves us in awe at the wonder of His love.

The season of Advent begins this Sunday. The Middle English word *advent* means an arrival or approach—the Latin prefix *ad* meaning toward and *ven* meaning to come.[1]

The celebration of someone special is coming.

Please join us as we celebrate the gift of His presence—that special silent night when God sent a baby to us, for us. It's time to prepare our hearts for the Holy One to come.

You will not want to miss this season.

Many Blessings,

Mindy Lee Hopman

Enter His gates
with thanksgiving
and His courts with praise.
Give thanks to Him,
bless His name.

~Psalm 100:4

hope

FIRST SUNDAY

Hope

Enter His gates with thanksgiving and His courts with praise.
Give thanks to Him, bless His name. ~Psalm 100:4

With grateful hearts filled with thanksgiving, we enter the season of Christmas to celebrate one special baby.

We prepare the tree, the home, and the presents.
We prepare our hearts to celebrate His presence.

We celebrate the presence of a baby sent to our world over 2,000 years ago who brings us together again as ONE in the same spiritual family tree.

In the beginning was the Word, and the Word was with God, and the Word was God. He was in the beginning with God. All things came into being through Him, and apart from Him nothing came into being that has come into being. In Him was life, and the life was the Light of men. ~John 1:1-4

Our hearts rejoice with HOPE as we await one great birthday celebration!

And the Word became flesh, and dwelt among us, and we saw His glory,
glory as of the only begotten from the Father, full of grace and truth.
~John 1:14

During this season of preparation, otherwise known as Advent, we take time to prepare our hearts by looking at our *Faith Roots*. Within the perfectly grafted tree, we find the beautiful legacy of our faith.

The beautiful legacy of our faith is found in the faith-family tree.

What else do we have to hold onto tightly with the headlines that surround us today?

The people who walk in darkness will see a great light;
those who live in a dark land, the light will shine on them. ~Isaiah 9:2

The Light shines for our eyes to see back to the beginning of time and for our hearts to look forward with everlasting hope.

For a child will be born to us, a son will be given to us; and the government will rest on His shoulders; and His name will be called Wonderful Counselor, Mighty God, Eternal Father, Prince of Peace. ~Isaiah 9:6

Today, the first Sunday of the Advent season, we light the candle of prophecy, otherwise known as the candle of HOPE.

Again Isaiah says, "There shall come the root of Jesse, and He who arises to rule over the Gentiles, in Him shall the Gentiles hope. Now may the God of hope fill you with all joy and peace in believing, so that you will abound in hope by the power of the Holy Spirit." ~Romans 15:12-13

With thankful hearts, we understand the depth of the season and we . . . slow . . . down. Because if we don't, we will miss it.

For the LORD is good; His lovingkindness is everlasting and His faithfulness to all generations. ~Psalm100:5

The spiritual seed passes down from you to the next generation when God passes down the greatest gift through you.

You don't want to miss this. I don't want to miss this. We don't want to be so distracted by the things of the world that we miss the true meaning of the season.

It is the greatest story ever told about the greatest gift ever given.

The story is about the light of HOPE who came down as a baby, who shines in a dark world, and who will come again one day.

Not everyone will slow down.
Not everyone will stop what they are doing.
Not everyone will recognize the Lord of lords and King of kings.
But the called, chosen, and faithful will follow.

With full, thankful hearts, we prepare to celebrate our Living Hope.

> *… who through him are believers in God, who raised him from the dead and gave him glory, so that your faith and hope are in God. ~1 Peter 1:21, NIV*

May we shift our focus from self to Savior.

Let's allow Him to love us as He brings us together as one family this Christmas season and fills our hearts with the gift of His presence, the wonder of His love, and His amazing grace.

This Advent season we make the conscious choice to slow down enough to bask in His Light. We take time to look back at our faith-family tree to see snapshots of our roots from the beginning of time as they lead up to the birth of our Savior.

Let's savor the season together.
Happy Sunday!

WEEK ONE
THE BIG PICTURE

Pristine beaches, snow-capped mountains, deserts, swamps, Lowcountry, Midlands, Upstate, the Everglades, rural farms abundant with crops, fast-paced, busy city streets and people scattered everywhere within and in-between. Take a look around. Do you marvel at God's goodness and awesomeness? From the design of the stars above to the design of the land and to the delicate design of our hearts, our Father—Creator of all and Master Designer—placed us here in love to love, but when did His love begin?

His love began at the beginning of time when God created the greatest love story.

Bereishit Bara Elohim, "In the beginning God created." To *bara* means to shape, to form, to create, or to give birth to something new. *Bereishit* means the beginning and *Elohim* is the name of our supreme God![2]

Every sunrise and sunset declares the majesty of His glorious creation!

It is as if my Heavenly Father swipes His glorious paintbrush, dipped in gold and red beauty, across the wide-open canvas just for my eyes to see. And the beauty of His presence settles my beating heart as I rest in knowing I am a part of His *big picture*, just as you are.

Bara Elohim, "God created" every day in a specific order with a strategic purpose. From creation to chaos to complete function, waters without limits and complete darkness were formed and fashioned to collaborate.[3]

Creation continues when conception causes each beating heart to come alive. The sweet cry heard as a baby enters the world melts a mama's heart. His creation overwhelmed my soul when each of my babies was placed in my arms for the first time.

After God created the world, He created families to live in the world in a community as one, from the beginning of time until the end of time.

day one

When we gather with those we love {family and friends} we feel complete. Our families are not perfect. We are all a little crazy, and every family contends with issues, but overall our love for each other runs deep. We have walked through good times and hard times together as one. Close friends who have joined us during different seasons have become our family, because when family isn't present, God provides people to fill the void of the missing members.

When we are one in the Spirit, we become family.

Oneness, created by God, is found in the complete family unit. Glimpses of our time together create the snapshots that fall within God's *big picture*.

■ Today's Scripture:

Elohim. God, Ruler, Judge, Creator. Genesis 1:1

> *In the beginning was the Word and the Word was with God, and the Word was God. ~John 1:1*

> *In the beginning God created the heavens and the earth. The earth was formless and void, and darkness was over the surface of the deep, and the Spirit of God was moving over the surface of the waters. ~Genesis 1:1-2*

> *He is the image of the invisible God, the firstborn of all creation. For by Him all things were created, both in the heavens and on earth, visible and invisible, whether thrones or dominions or rulers or authorities—all things have been created through Him and for Him. He is before all things, and in Him all things hold together. ~Colossians 1:15-17*

> *He also says to the Son, "In the beginning, Lord, you laid the foundation of the earth and made the heavens with your hands." ~Hebrews 1:10, NLT*

God created the world, and He holds His precious creation in the palm of His hand.

■ Today's Snapshot: The Big Picture

The Father, the Son, and the Holy Spirit captivated creation in its fullness and completeness. From the darkness and light to each plant and tree on the ground, to each egg in the nests, to the birds in the sky, to the fish in the ocean, to the animals on dry land—perfection was achieved in creation. God thrives in oneness. God did not dwell alone. The Father, the Son, and the Holy Spirit dwelt in oneness and perfection together. Our Heavenly Father loves community!

Relationships nestled within the Old Testament {great dads, moms, grandparents, uncles/aunts, and children, as well as some not-so-great ones} appear as snapshots within God's *big picture*. There are snapshots of oneness as well as snapshots of brokenness in our faith-family tree. Regardless of how complete or broken each family appears, every snapshot of this story plays an important role in God's *big picture*.

As we focus on the birth of Christ, the snapshots display family photos which originated in the beginning of time and move right into the arms of the young mother who gave birth to the Savior of the world, to today. He was with the Father, then He returned to bring us back to the Father.

The baby born over 2,000 years ago came to mend brokenness and establish oneness again. This baby brought hope to a hurting world. This season, we celebrate the baby who was born for one purpose—to make brokenness complete.

■ Today's Family Discussion:
- What is your favorite Christmas tradition?
- Is there a new tradition you would like to start this year?

■ Closing Prayer:
Heavenly Father,
We praise You for who You are—The Creator and Master Designer. You created the world, and You created each one of us to come together as one. Our family fits perfectly into Your **big picture**. *Gratefully, we see a glimpse of the* **big picture** *through Your family snapshots. Thank You for sharing the snapshots of Your story with us. Thank You for helping us to see how the snapshots of our stories fit perfectly into The Greatest Story. May You continue to guide our family through this Advent season as we slow down and focus on the reason for this beautiful season. In the precious name of Jesus we pray, Amen*

OUR HEAVENLY FATHER

A few years ago, Hurricane Matthew hit the island of Hilton Head in the Lowcountry of South Carolina. Water surrounded our home and poured into the crawl space. Tall pine trees tumbled like toothpicks, debris scattered everywhere, and boats floated right off of docks and landed in yards and golf courses! For months afterward, blue tarps covered the homes whose shingles had been ripped off, and we watched FEMA trucks pick up logs, branches, and root balls from the mountainous piles that sat along the roadside.

One year later, Hurricane Irma hit Hilton Head Island. While the wind didn't do nearly as much damage as Hurricane Matthew, the high water levels were destructive to low-lying homes. The hurricane hit at high tide which flooded the streets. My children kayaked right down our road! This past September, Hurricane Florence flew in at high force, but God's presence was more powerful than even the hurricane force winds!

You might deal with snow/ice storms, tsunamis, or even earthquakes where you live. Regardless, every natural disaster takes us by surprise, even though God knows when the storm is on its way. Nothing is a surprise to our omniscient {all-knowing} God.

Our God is not a distant Father from the days of old; although He was present in the past, He is also a part of our present.

God loved us before creation. He created each one of us for the purpose of carrying out His plan. He is the Author of our stories.

Everyone needs the presence of a caring father to encourage and love our souls throughout the span of our stories.

Just as an earthly father {who is present} cares, nurtures, and protects his children, and will do everything he can to protect his family during the storm, God {who is omnipresent—always present everywhere} does the same for us. In an ideal situation, some will see glimpses of our Heavenly Father in our earthly fathers.

Regardless of the situation with your earthly father, your Heavenly Father is always present because He is unlimited by time or space. He never gets distracted. He is never too busy to listen. He is actively engaged in each of our lives. He hopes we choose to be still in Him and let Him turn the next page of our stories.

God wants us to trust Him in the good times and let Him turn the pages so that our roots are anchored in our faith when life's storms arrive. And they will arrive.

When each major storm comes to us, hope is the anchor of our souls.

We can trust the Creator of all things created.

We can trust the One who intimately knows us and loves us more than we can imagine.

We can trust that our stories will be woven into His story, which is the greatest story of all time. So we hold on tight, and when He brings us through to the other side, we praise Him for His presence before, during, and after the storm.

■ **Today's Scripture:**
Abba. Daddy. Romans 8:15

> *For you have not received a spirit of slavery leading to fear again, but you have received a spirit of adoption as sons by which we cry out, "Abba! Father!"*
> *~Romans 8:15*

day two

This hope we have as an anchor of the soul, a hope both sure and steadfast and one which enters within the veil, where Jesus has entered as a forerunner for us, having become a high priest forever according to the order of Melchizedek.
~Hebrews 6:19-20

… fixing our eyes on Jesus, the author, and perfecter of faith.
~Hebrews 12:2a

Jesus Christ is the same yesterday and today and forever. ~Hebrews 13:8

Because you are sons, God has sent forth the Spirit of His Son into our hearts, crying, "Abba! Father!" ~Galatians 4:6

■ Today's Snapshot: Our Heavenly Father
He was. He is. And He is to come.

Our Heavenly Father has always been present—yesterday, today, and tomorrow; and He loved us first. As a parent loves a child from the thought of conception, God loved us unconditionally from the beginning. He is our Creator, He is the Author of our story, and He is the Lover of our soul.

■ Today's Family Discussion:
- What is unconditional love? Do you love anyone or anything unconditionally?
- Do you realize that God, your Heavenly Father, is also the Author of your story? How exciting!
- What do you think your next chapter will be?

■ Closing Prayer:
Heavenly Father,
Thank You for loving each one of us first. Thank You for creating us perfectly and for sending Your Son to die for us so that we can all come together as one again. We are grateful. As we enter into this Christmas season with hearts full of hope, may we continue to experience the wonder of Your amazing love. You are a good Father, and we are grateful.
In the precious name of Jesus we pray, Amen

THE FIRST HUSBAND & WIFE

In the beginning, completeness in spirit and wholeness of heart existed in one place. *Elohim bara* the world. *Elohim bara Adam*, God the Father, God the Son, and God the Holy Spirit together created man in their image. *Elohim*, God with a plural ending, created man, and out of man's rib *Elohim* created woman.

As a young bride, I remember how his eyes bore straight to my soul when I started to walk down the aisle. In just twenty paces, I would say my vows and become his wife. The memory of him looking at me with such tenderness will forever be etched on my heart.

The marriage covenant is a glimpse of the beginning when Adam and Eve lived as one with God and of the future when Christ unites as one with the church.

Photographer Haylee Lynn Hopman

With His hands He created the world.
With His heart He created you.

God fashioned you and your spouse perfectly. God gave each of you life, imparted a soul to your beings at conception, and gave His masterpieces the perfect eyes, smiles, and laughs to be joined together as one.

Does your soul know it well? When your soul knows it well, you accept you are fearfully and wonderfully made and you are able to see the beauty of oneness in marriage when bound together by God.

And if one can overpower him who is alone, two can resist him. A cord of three strands is not quickly torn apart. ~Ecclesiastes 4:12

day three

■ **Today's Scripture:**

Then God said, "Let Us make man in Our image,"... male and female He created them. ~Genesis 1:26-27

Then the LORD God formed man of dust from the ground, and breathed into his nostrils the breath of life; and man became a living being. ~Genesis 2:7

For You formed my inward parts; You wove me in my mother's womb. I will give thanks to You, for I am fearfully and wonderfully made; Wonderful are Your works, and my soul knows it very well. ~Psalm 139:13-14

For we are His workmanship, created in Christ Jesus for good works, which God prepared beforehand so that we would walk in them. ~Ephesians 2:10

Then the Lord God said, "It is not good for the man to be alone; I will make him a helper suitable for him." Out of the ground the Lord God formed every beast of the field and every bird of the sky, and brought them to the man to see what he would call them; and whatever the man called a living creature, that was its name. The man gave names to all the cattle, and to the birds of the sky, and to every beast of the field, but for Adam there was not found a helper suitable for him. So the Lord God caused a deep sleep to fall upon the man, and he slept; then He took one of his ribs and closed up the flesh at that place. The Lord God fashioned into a woman the rib which He had taken from the man, and brought her to the man. The man said, "This is now bone of my bones, And flesh of my flesh; She shall be called Woman, Because she was taken out of Man." For this reason a man shall leave his father and his mother, and be joined to his wife; and they shall become one flesh. And the man and his wife were both naked and were not ashamed. ~Genesis 2:18-25

I will rejoice greatly in the LORD, My soul will exult in my God; For He has clothed me with garments of salvation, He has wrapped me with a robe of righteousness, as a bridegroom decks himself with a garland, and as a bride adorns herself with her jewels. ~Isaiah 61:10

Let us rejoice and be glad and give the glory to Him, for the marriage of the Lamb has come and His bride has made herself ready. ~Revelation 19:7

■ Today's Snapshot: The First Husband and Wife

God looked over all of His creation and said, "It is good." And it was, until God realized that it was not good for man to be alone. Our Heavenly Father knows what is best for His children, and He wants what is best for us. So, God created a companion for Adam out of his rib, whom He named Eve. Adam was the father, and Eve was the mother of all living. They lived together in community with God in the Garden of Eden.

■ Family Discussion:

- We all belong to God. List the people closest to you —your community?
- Describe your wedding day to your children {where, when, who was there, etc.}. If you are not married, describe what the perfect wedding day would look like for you.

Every person may not get married. Remaining single is a special calling given to some people. Together, all believers are one body called the bride of Christ who is preparing herself for marriage to the Lamb (Revelation 19:7-8).

■ Closing Prayer:

Heavenly Father, We praise You for the creation of the world, all the animals, and for Adam, the first man. He gives us a glimpse of You. And we praise You for Eve. Adam and Eve are the perfect picture of marriage. We thank You for the gift of marriage—a commitment to love, to honor, and to sacrifice. May our marriage and the marriage of each one of our children be built upon Your firm foundation. May the body of believers unite as one to prepare for the marriage to the Lamb in which we have victory and eternal fellowship. Thank You for these sweet moments to remind us of Your everlasting love for us. In the precious name of Jesus we pray, Amen

THE BROKEN HEART

Today's headlines reek of terrorist attacks, shootings in our country, hurricanes, and wildfires. Researchers continue to look hard for cures, while sickness still abounds. Bullying runs rampant in America. Thoughts of suicide and cutting are prevalent among teenagers, because self-esteem is low, and worldly success weighs heavily on the shoulders of children in this culture like a ton of bricks. Not to mention, families are falling to pieces. Our world hurts today.

It wasn't like this in the beginning.

In the beginning, the world was beautifully perfect. Adam and Eve dwelt with God in the Garden of Eden. They lived together as one. God gave Adam and Eve free will so that they {mankind} would choose to worship Him. God gave His children great freedom, but He also gave them one rule for their own safety and protection.

The LORD God commanded the man, saying, "From any tree of the garden you may eat freely; but from the tree of the knowledge of good and evil you shall not eat, for in the day that you eat from it you will surely die." ~Genesis 2:16-17

They only had one rule.

Since the beginning of time, the adversary has been out to deceive mankind, to pull us away from God. Adam and Eve chose to go their way and not listen to the Father. Pride moved in, they ate the forbidden fruit, unity was split, and they broke our Heavenly Father's heart.

■ **Today's Scripture:**

The man said, "The woman whom You gave to be with me, she gave me from the tree and I ate." Then the LORD God said to the woman, "What is this you have done?" And the woman said, "The serpent deceived me, and I ate." ~Genesis 3:12-13

And I will put enmity between you and the woman, And between your seed and her seed; He shall bruise you on the head, and you shall bruise him on the heel." ~Genesis 3:15

day four

For the grace of God has appeared, bringing salvation to all men, instructing us to deny ungodliness and worldly desires and to live sensibly, righteously and godly in the present age, looking for the blessed hope and the appearing of the glory of our great God and Savior, Christ Jesus, who gave Himself for us to redeem us from every lawless deed, and to purify for Himself a people for His own possession, zealous for good deeds. ~Titus 2:11-14

...and He will wipe away every tear from their eyes; and there will no longer be any death; there will no longer be any mourning, or crying, or pain; the first things have passed away. And He who sits on the throne said, "Behold, I am making all things new." And He said, "Write, for these words are faithful and true." ~Revelation 21:4-5

■ Today's Snapshot: The Broken Heart

God told Adam and Eve they could eat from any tree in the Garden of Eden except the tree of the knowledge of good and evil. Adam and Eve, deceived by the lie of the enemy, chose to eat the forbidden fruit because pride slipped in when they believed the lie that they could be wise like God. They did the one thing God asked them not to do. As a parent's heart breaks when a child decides to go his or her own way, God's heart must have felt the same way.

The consequence of Adam and Eve's sin was to leave the Garden of Eden and become subject to death. They were broken away from oneness with God and became eternally separated from God. Consequently, we the descendants of Adam, at that moment, were also broken away from oneness with God and we became eternally separated from God.

If our world wasn't broken, we wouldn't need a Savior to mend it back together again.

While Adam introduced sin; Jesus is the antidote for sin. God sent baby Jesus into the world to redeem us and restore our oneness with God. The birth of Christ became our blessed hope in the manger over 2,000 years ago, and the death and resurrection of Christ made salvation from sin available for all.

O come, O come, Emmanuel

And ransom captive Israel

That mourns in lonely exile here

Until the Son of God appears

Rejoice! Rejoice! Emmanuel

Shall come to thee, O Israel

     ~ John Mason Neale (1818-1866)

■ **Family Discussion:**
- Do you think Adam and Eve regretted the choice they made? When have you made a choice that you regretted?
- God forgave Adam and Eve and then sent us a baby for Christmas to redeem us. Since God forgives you, are you able to forgive others easily?
- Take a few moments for silent confession to God.

     If we confess our sins, He is faithful and righteous to forgive us our sins and to cleanse us from all unrighteousness. ~1 John 1:9

■ **Closing Prayer:**
     Heavenly Father,
     We praise You for giving us the gift of free will. We freely choose to praise You! We praise You for the baby whom You sent to mend our hurting world. We praise You for placing Your Son on the cross for each one of us. On the cross, we find forgiveness and redemption through the blood of Jesus. But Jesus overcame death, and in Him, one day so will we! Help us to keep our eyes on You, our Living Hope, dear Jesus.
     In the precious name of Jesus we pray, Amen

THE BLESSINGS

There is something special about your name.

When Hunter and Haylee attended Lower School, I worked in the Lower School building. Normally they walked to my classroom at the end of the day, but on a rare occasion when someone else picked them up from school in the car line, they enjoyed sitting with the rest of the children and listening quietly for their names to be called over the intercom. My daughter loved hearing her name called out loud! The sound of her name made her squeal with delight.

Our names are special because they are our identity. Many significant names play different roles in the lineage of Jesus.

Several generations after Adam and Eve, the people began to do evil in the eyes of the Lord. God saw the wickedness of man and it grieved His heart. He decided to destroy all the living things, except for two of every animal and the family of a man named Noah. Noah was the exception. He found favor with God.

Noah's name means "rest or relief" and amongst Noah's peers and family, his identity came from God. Noah did what was right in the sight of God, so God used one righteous man to preserve the animals and to save mankind. When God destroyed the world by water, God let Noah rest in Him. And once Noah's family stood on dry ground again, snapshots of the faith-family tree continued to travel through Noah's oldest son, Shem. From Shem's name, which means "name" comes our identity.[4]

From the animals on the ark to the animals in the manger to the baby who was renowned for all mankind, Noah's faithful heart played a part in it all.

■ **Today's Scripture:**

Every good thing given and every perfect gift is from above, coming down from the Father of lights, with whom there is no variation or shifting shadow. ~James 1:17

But Noah found favor in the eyes of the Lord. These are the records of the generations of Noah. Noah was a righteous man, blameless in his time; Noah walked with God. Noah became the father of three sons: Shem, Ham, and Japheth. Now the earth was corrupt in the sight of God, and the earth was filled with violence. ~Genesis 6:9-11

Then God told Noah and his sons, "I hereby confirm my covenant with you and your descendants, and with all the animals that were on the boat with you—the birds, the livestock, and all the wild animals—every living creature on earth. Yes, I am confirming my covenant with you. Never again will floodwaters kill all living creature; never again will a flood destroy the earth."

Then God said, "I am giving you a sign of my covenant with you and with all living creature, for all generations to come. I have placed my rainbow in the clouds. It is the sign of my covenant with you and with the earth." ~Genesis 9:8-13

By faith Noah, when warned about things not yet seen, in holy fear built an ark to save his family. By his faith he condemned the world and became heir of the righteousness that is in keeping with faith. ~Hebrews 11:7 NIV

day five

■ **Today's Snapshot: The Blessings**

Generations after God created Adam and Eve, once again God's heart was grieved. Man had gone his own way and placed his focus on the creation instead of the Creator. God decided to destroy the world by water. God saw integrity inside Noah's confident heart, so He used Noah for the mighty job of preserving the animals and mankind. He asked Noah to build an ark and place two of every creature in the ark--male and female. Then God sent the waters. The waters destroyed God's creation, but through the destruction, God used Noah's faithful family to preserve a lineage for the coming of the Promised One, and by Noah's son Shem we are named in the faith-family tree.

Noah trusted God and rested in Him through the storm.

After the great flood, peace prevailed when the King-of-kings was born among a sweet group of animals, who were preserved generations earlier for that perfect first Christmas.

■ **Family Discussion:**
- Which animal would you love to be for a day?
- Noah had many pets. What do you think it was like being on a ship filled with every animal of the world? Amazing or Stinky?
- What was special about Noah's heart? Why did God choose him?

■ **Closing Prayer:**
Heavenly Father,
We praise You for giving us unique names that represent our identity. We also praise You for the animals you created. Each kind is beautiful in its own special way. Thank You for preserving us through the righteous heart of Noah when You destroyed the world by water. Thank you for the sweet pictures You give us of the animals in the manger who witnessed the birth of a King in their home. From the ark to the cross, may our hearts rest in Your protection and guidance. May we have hearts like Noah, which are righteous and full of integrity and devotion towards You. Thank You for this Christmas season when we confidently prepare our hearts and await the coming of the King!
In the precious name of Jesus we pray, Amen

THE BEAUTIFUL LEGACY

My grandfather and I had the best talks. I'm pretty sure it's because he spoke straight to my heart. He shared stories about the Jewish traditions he followed in his Orthodox home and the traditions he continued to follow up until the day he passed away. Regardless of what we were talking about, my grandfather always made me feel special. I knew he delighted in me because he told me he did. And oh, how I loved him.

One day we were talking side-by-side when he leaned over and whispered *naches*. I looked at him with my wide eyes, passed down from his generation to mine, and I questioned him. He said, "*Naches* is a Yiddish term which describes the feelings of joy that a child brings to a parent." He continued, "When the joy is so great it exceeds your words, you use the term *naches*."

day six

I knew the feeling. I'd felt it before.

It's the joy a parent feels when a child does something unexpected for someone else or surprises the parent by going above and beyond what you asked him or her to do. When words cannot express the delight you feel, you know you have experienced *naches*.

As I watched my Grandfather watch my children, I understood. Grandchildren bring *naches* to their grandparents just because of who they are, not because of anything they do!

In the Old Testament, a man named Terah descended several generations later from Noah's son Shem. Terah did not have a heart for God like Noah, but Terah's son Abram loved God. God asked Abram to follow Him out of the metropolis of Ur into an unknown land.

God said to let go of your past and let Me lead you.
Does this sound familiar?

God uses people from all walks of life who have a heart for Him.

Abram had a heart for God—God promised Abram that he would be the father of many nations, He would give them land, and He would be their God.

Then God cut an everlasting covenant, or made an agreement, with Abram and changed Abram's name to Abraham and Sarai's name to Sarah. God changed their lives and He gave them new names.

> **When God makes you a promise,**
> **you have to know in your heart of hearts that**
> **He will follow through,**
> **because God keeps His promises.**

Abraham, a great Patriarch in the faith-family tree, became the father of Isaac, the grandfather of Jacob—whom we will later know as Israel. Through the good and the not-so-good times, they all followed God and they brought Him *naches*.

■ **Today's Scripture:** *YHWH Jireh.* The Lord will Provide. Genesis 22:14

Now the LORD said to Abram, "Go forth from your country, and from your relatives and from your father's house, to the land which I will show you; and I will make you a great nation, and I will bless you; and make your name great; and so you shall be a blessing; and I will bless those who bless you, and the one who curses you I will curse, and in you all the families of the earth will be blessed." ~Genesis 12:1-3

And He took him outside and said, "Now look toward the heavens, and count the stars, if you are able to count them." And He said to him, "So shall your descendants be." ~Genesis 15:5

Then the LORD took note of Sarah as He had said, and the LORD did for Sarah as He had promised. So Sarah conceived and bore a son to Abraham in his old age at the appointed time of which God had spoken to him. ~Genesis 21:1-2

He said, "Do not stretch out your hand against the lad, and do nothing to him; for now I know that you fear God, since you have not withheld your son, your only son, from Me." Then Abraham raised his eyes and looked, and behold, behind him a ram caught in the thicket by his horns; and Abraham went and took the ram and offered him up for a burnt offering in the place of his son. Abraham called the name of that place The LORD Will Provide, [Hebrew YHWH-jireh] as it is said to this day, "In the mount of the LORD it will be provided." ~Genesis 22:12-14

For my thoughts are not your thoughts, neither are your ways my ways," declares the Lord. "As the heavens are higher than the earth, so are my ways higher than your ways and my thoughts than your thoughts. ~Isaiah 55:8-9, NIV

■ **Today's Snapshot: The Beautiful Legacy**
God told Abram to go, and Abram let God lead Him. He left the metropolis of Ur and headed to a land unknown to his wife Sarai and his nephew Lot. When God asks you to do something, you have to trust Him, because God can see the *big picture*, while we can only see a snapshot of time.

- God established His covenant with Abram (Genesis 17:2).
- God promised Abram He would multiply him exceedingly, and he would be a father of many nations (Genesis 17:4-5).
- God sealed the promise and changed Abram's name and Sarai's name to Abraham and Sarah to show that God was with them (Genesis 17:5, 15).
- God promised Abraham a great land (Genesis 17:8).
- God promised Abraham a son by Sarah (Genesis 17:16).
- God made these promises to Abraham when he was 99 years old, and Sarah was 90 (Genesis 17:1,17).

These promises that did not make sense to man could only be fulfilled by God.

Promises are meant to be kept.
God keeps His promises.

Sometimes this is difficult to remember because we think God views promises as we do. As human beings, we try to keep our promises, but sometimes life gets in the way. When God makes you a promise, He will not become distracted, overwhelmed, or pressured in a different direction. Life will not become too difficult, and time will not get in the way of keeping the promise. Regardless of what is going on around Him, God will stay focused on the promise He made.

And He will keep that promise.

Over time, God established trust with Abraham.

God tested Abraham's faith when He asked Abraham to sacrifice his one and only son as a burnt offering. When God asked Abraham to sacrifice Isaac on the altar, Abraham proved that he truly feared God. Abrahams obedient heart led God to provide a ram in the thicket to take the place of Isaac who was tied on the altar. Abraham trusted and followed God and Abraham must have brought God great *naches*.

When you cannot see or do not understand,
you can trust that God keeps His promises.

In God's perfect timing God provided His own baby one holy night who would become the final sacrifice on an old rugged cross, once and for all.

**When we trust Him and follow Him,
we bring our Heavenly Father *naches*.**

■ **Family Discussion:**
- Has someone broken a promise to you before? How did it make you feel?
- Discuss a time when it was hard to trust your parents, elders or someone special to you, or God. Afterward, were you glad you you placed your trust in that person?
- In the future, when might you have to display this same kind of trust?

■ **Closing Prayer:**
Heavenly Father,
We praise You for Your Fatherly love. Thank You for always knowing what is best for us, and for always keeping Your promises. May we walk confidently knowing that Your ways are better than ours because You can see the big picture. May we rest in the fullness of our trust in You because You know each one of us so well. Thank You for the grandparents in our lives who show this love to us. We are so grateful. You knew we needed a Savior, so You sent One. You sent us a baby who was fully God, yet fully man. You knew we would be celebrating His birth for years to come. Thank You for the gentle reminder of Your great love. May we continue to trust You in our individual lives and may we bring You great joy. In the precious name of Jesus we pray, Amen

And the *peace* of God, which surpasses all comprehension, will guard your hearts and your minds in Christ Jesus. *~Philippians 4:7*

peace

SECOND SUNDAY

Peace

And the peace of God, which surpasses all comprehension, will guard your hearts and your minds in Christ Jesus. ~Philippians 4:7

...the word of God came to John son of Zechariah in the wilderness. He went into all the country around the Jordan, preaching a baptism of repentance for the forgiveness of sins. As it is written in the book of the words of Isaiah the prophet: "A voice of one calling in the wilderness, 'Prepare the way for the Lord, make straight paths for him. Every valley shall be filled in, every mountain and hill made low. The crooked roads shall become straight, the rough ways smooth. And all people will see God's salvation.' "
~Luke 3:2b-6, NIV

May we prepare the way for the Lord by preparing our hearts for His coming, and we need Him to come. When words cannot heal broken hearts, we realize we need the Word.

The Word brings PEACE. Peace is the presence of God.

> **When words cannot make sad hearts happy again,**
> **we realize we need the Word.**

In the beginning was the Word, and the Word was with God, and the Word was God. ~John 1:1

And the Word became flesh, and dwelt among us, and we saw His glory, glory as of the only begotten from the Father, full of grace and truth. ~John 1:14

From God, through the womb of a woman, the Word became flesh and dwelt among us. Jesus was fully God, yet fully man. He came to show love, kindness, and mercy to a hurting world. He came to give grace. Jesus came to offer peace to a hurting world.

> *But he was pierced for our transgressions, he was crushed for our iniquities; the punishment that brought us peace was on him, and by his wounds we are healed. ~Isaiah 53:5, NIV*

By His wounds, we are healed. God offered forgiveness to a hurting world through the sacrifice of His Son. When we turn back to Him, we make room for the peace of God to enter our hearts. The Word is the place where peace for hurting hearts is found.

> *For it was the Father's good pleasure for all the fullness to dwell in Him, and through Him to reconcile all things to Himself, having made peace through the blood of His cross; through Him, I say, whether things on earth or things in heaven. ~Colossians 1:19-20*

His presence brings PEACE to our hearts.
His presence is God's present to the world.

On this second Sunday of Advent, we light a candle for peace.
May your heart find peace in Him. He came for you.

> *Yet to all who did receive him, to those who believed in his name, he gave the right to become children of God—children born not of natural descent, nor of human decision or a husband's will, but born of God. ~John 1:12-13, NIV*

Receive, believe, and become a child of God. The Father gave peace to His children's hearts when He sent His Son into our world to redeem us, and in Him peace is found today.

> *The people walking in darkness have seen a great light; on those living in the land of deep darkness a light has dawned. ~Isaiah 9:2, NIV*

> *For a child will be born to us, a son will be given to us; and the government will rest on His shoulders; And His name will be called Wonderful Counselor, Mighty God, Eternal Father, Prince of Peace. ~Isaiah 9:6*

God with us ~ Immanuel ~ Peace has come

There will be no end to the increase of His government or of peace. On the throne of David and over his kingdom, to establish it and to uphold it with justice and righteousness from then on and forevermore. The zeal of the LORD of hosts will accomplish this. ~Isaiah 9:7

Peace I leave with you; my peace I give to you. Not as the world gives do I give to you. Let not your hearts be troubled, neither let them be afraid. ~John 14:27, ESV

Because of the tender mercy of our God, with which the Sunrise from on high will visit us, to shine upon those who sit in darkness and the shadow of death, to guide our feet into the way of peace. ~Luke 1:78-79

God gives the greatest gifts. On Christmas, He gave us the gift of His Son who offers grace and peace to this hurting world.

What child is this, who laid to rest

On Mary's lap is sleeping?

Whom angels greet with anthems sweet,

While shepherds watch are keeping?

This, this is Christ the King,

Whom shepherds guard and Angels sing;

Haste, haste to bring Him laud,

The Babe, the Son of Mary.

~William Chatterton Dix (1865)

May the peace which transcends all understanding fill your hearts today. Happy Sunday!

WEEK TWO
THE TUMULTUOUS TWINS

Every time a child is born, we rejoice! And it's twice as nice when we celebrate the birth of twins! My daughter Haylee and I love watching Hayley Mills go away to camp in *The Parent Trap* where she finds her twin. The movie's excitement grows as the girls switch roles to go to each other's home and get to know the other parent! My experiences with twins extend to those I have taught, to twins of my close friends and family, to twins who live right down the street. The dynamics of twins is always exciting!

Here are a few fun facts about twins:
1. Having two babies at one time is linked to a mother living longer.
2. Even though twins may trick their parents sometimes, they never trick a dog!
3. Identical twins do not have identical fingerprints!
4. Identical twins do share 99% of each other's genes!
5. Twins begin communicating with each other in the womb.[5]

From the lineage of the patriarch Abraham came the blessing of Isaacs' twins.

■ **Today's Scripture:**

The LORD said to her, "Two nations are in your womb; And two peoples will be separated from your body; And one people shall be stronger than the other; And the older shall serve the younger." ~Genesis 25:23

Now it came about, when Isaac was old and his eyes were too dim to see, that he called his older son Esau and said to him, "My son." And he said to him, "Here I am." ~Genesis 27:1

Rebekah was listening while Isaac spoke to his son Esau. So when Esau went to the field to hunt for game to bring home, Rebekah said to her son Jacob, "Behold, I heard your father speak to your brother Esau, saying, 'Bring me some game and prepare a savory dish for me, that I may eat, and bless you in the presence of the LORD before my death.'" ~Genesis 27:5-7

day one

"...Go out to the flock and bring me two choice young goats, so I can prepare some tasty food for your father, just the way he likes it." ~Genesis 27:9, NIV
By faith, Isaac blessed Jacob and Esau in regard to their future.
~Hebrews 11:20, NIV

■ Today's Snapshot: The Tumultuous Twins

Isaac {Abraham's son} and Rebekah were not blessed with babies at the beginning of their marriage. However, Isaac knew the promise God made to Abraham. God made Abraham a promise that included thousands upon thousands of descendants—more numerous than the stars in the sky! So, Isaac prayed for Rebekah, and God blessed them with two sons.

Esau entered the world before his brother, Jacob, thus earning the birthright of the firstborn son.

God continued to bring forth the Messiah through a bloodline which included deceit, trickery, and lies.

While Jacob stayed among the tents and became Rebekah's favorite, Esau was an avid hunter which pleased his father immensely. One day, Esau came inside famished after a hard day of hunting. He could smell Jacob's savory stew on the stove. Esau asked for some of the red lentil stew. Jacob told him he could have a bowl of stew in exchange for his birthright, and Esau traded his birthright for one meal!
In the custom of the time the firstborn received:

> *...a double share of all he has. That son is the first sign of his father's strength. The right of the firstborn belongs to him.*
> *~Deuteronomy 21:17, NIV*

Esau took his eyes off of the *big picture* for temporary satisfaction when he gave Jacob his birthright in exchange for one bowl of stew. Then Rebekah helped Jacob deceive Isaac to receive the blessing.

From a human perspective, the lineage of Jesus Christ would have traveled through the bloodline of Esau.

From a heavenly perspective, the spiritual Seed moves through the younger son, Jacob.

It happened that quickly.

One shallow choice equaled one eternal shift in the Savior's lineage.

Could moments which seem deceptive actually be divine?

In God's sovereignty—through what appears to us as a human betrayal—Jacob received the birthright, and then—through one act of human deceit—Jacob received the blessing from Isaac.

■ **Family Discussion:**
- What would be the best thing about having a twin? What would be the worst thing about having a twin?
- Why is it important to keep our eyes on the *big picture*? How can this help us when we make decisions?

■ **Closing Prayer:**
Heavenly Father,
We praise You for the gift of twins! We praise You for Esau and Jacob who help us to see that people in the Bible are real people who deal with real issues such as jealousy, deceit, and strife. You used their selfish actions to carry out Your eternal plan. Lord, thank You for loving us in spite of our flaws. Your beautiful plan is beginning to unfold, and we have the privilege of watching the story through snapshots of the **big picture**. *Thank You for giving us a glimpse into Your heart this Christmas as we anxiously await the birth of Your Son.*
In the precious name of Jesus we pray, Amen

A STRONG UNCLE

Wrestling is one sport that is whole-body, fierce, and intense, and it is the sport that my father and my brother loved. My father wrestled in college, and my brother wrestled from a little boy through the state level in high school. We watched his matches and yelled loudly, "Get him! Pin him!" He cut weight, so he was lean, and his strength could be seen in every muscle fiber of his body as he fought hard all the way through to the pin! When the wrestling match was finally over, we celebrated the thrill of the victory! Whew, it was intense!

That strong wrestler now serves with his family in the United States Marine Corps, and my kids love their "Tio Tommy!" They know he loves them because of the special attention he gives them when we are together. Our family adores his family, and we are grateful for the sacrifices they make for our country.

Uncles love their nieces and nephews in a special way.

Jacob and Esau, separated for over twenty years, both married and had children. Jacob went to see Esau. However, he wondered with great concern how Esau would react to him, his wives, and his children.

So Jacob sought God, and God met him in a heavenly wrestling match.

■ **Today's Scripture:**
El Shaddai. God Almighty. Psalm 91:1

> *So Jacob was left alone, and a man wrestled with him till daybreak.*
> *When the man saw that he could not overpower him, he touched the socket*
> *of Jacob's hip so that his hip was wrenched as he wrestled with the man.*
> *Then the man said, "Let me go, for it is daybreak."*
> *But Jacob replied, "I will not let you go unless you bless me."*
> *The man asked him,*
> *"What is your name?"*
> *"Jacob," he answered.*

day two

*Then the man said, "Your name will no longer be Jacob, but Israel,
because you have struggled with God and with humans and have overcome."
Jacob said, "Please tell me your name."
But he replied, "Why do you ask my name?"
Then he blessed him there.
So Jacob called the place Peniel, saying,
"It is because I saw God face to face, and yet my life was spared."
~Genesis 32:24-30, NIV*

*But he said to me, "My grace is sufficient for you, for my power is made perfect
in weakness." Therefore I will boast all the more gladly about my weaknesses, so
that Christ's power may rest on me.
~2 Corinthians 12:9, NIV*

*He who dwells in the shelter of the Most High will abide in the shadow of the
Almighty. ~Psalm 91:1*

■ Today's Snapshot: A Strong Uncle

Jacob spent the night seeking God before he met with Esau, knowing that he had received the blessing from Isaac, his father. Jacob knew that through his lineage {from Abraham through Isaac to him} his people would be multiplied greatly, he would continue to father many nations, and they would receive the Promised Land.

Jacob's head knew the truth, but his heart was anxious. When Jacob was alone, a figure approached him, and they began to wrestle fiercely throughout the night. In the conflict, the figure struck him hard in the thigh. The sinew of the thigh is made of cartilage and is strong as it holds the leg to the body. *God struck Jacob to make him weak so that in his weakness, Jacob would have to solely rely on God.* Jacob did not lose focus and God blessed him.

**In the struggle, we see God's presence, and we feel God's presence,
because in the struggle we need God's presence.**

As a sign of God's power being perfected in Jacob's weakness, God changed Jacob's name to Israel. After the wrestle, Jacob's heart rested in the promise. When Esau saw Jacob, the brothers ran to each other, embraced, and wept.

We can imagine how the children then rejoiced in their uncle's attention.

After the wrestle—
the wonder of His love and the fingerprints of His presence appear.

■ **Family Discussion:**
- Do you have a favorite uncle or someone who is like an uncle to you?
- Have you ever been so depleted of physical strength that you had to completely rely on God for strength? If so, explain.
- How did it feel for Him to get you to a point where you had to completely rely on Him?

■ **Closing Prayer:**
Heavenly Father,
We praise You for family and for uncles who love our children as their own. We praise You for the great wrestling match because we know that in You there is a victory at the end. Help us, Lord, to keep our focus on You when we are in the middle of the struggle. Please give us endurance as You bring us through, so that we may see the wonder of Your love. Help us see Your fingerprints and hold on fast to our hope in You. Thank You for the struggles Mary and Joseph overcame to bring Your Son into this world. We are forever grateful.
In the precious name of Jesus we pray, Amen

THE BOLD BROTHERS

Snow blanketed the sidewalks and streets in early January. We woke up to a winter wonderland and the kids jumped for joy as they stepped into their boots, placed their hands in their mittens, and put on their brightly colored jackets! Small and large children were shoveling, sledding, and playing in the snow, and their smiles were huge! Unexpected snow days are tons of fun! The children's coats were warm, bright, and made of many colors.

In the Old Testament, Israel gave Joseph a coat of many colors. Israel loved his son Joseph, who was born to him in his old age by his beloved wife, Rachael. But Joseph's half-brothers were extremely jealous of their father's affection towards him. Not only was Joseph the favored child, but he also garnered attention because of his crazy dreams! In one dream Joseph saw his brothers bowing down to him. A combination of the coat and the dream fueled the brothers' jealousy to the point they wanted to kill their younger sibling!

Leah's son Reuben, the oldest brother, suggested that the brothers sell Joseph instead of killing him. So, they threw Joseph into a pit and sold him into slavery. While Joseph was working as a slave, he never lost his confidence in God. But his integrity got him thrown into prison! After another series of events, he ended up in the Egyptian palace.

■ **Today's Scripture:**

The Lord was with Joseph so that he prospered, and he lived in the house of his Egyptian master. ~Genesis 39:2, NIV

Then Pharaoh said to Joseph, "Since God has made all this known to you, there is no one so discerning and wise as you. You shall be in charge of my palace, and all my people are to submit to your orders. Only with respect to the throne will I be greater than you." ~Genesis 41:39-40, NIV

"... But God sent me ahead of you to preserve for you a remnant on earth and to save your lives by a great deliverance." ~Genesis 45:7, NIV

"You intended to harm me, but God intended it for good to accomplish what is now being done, the saving of many lives." ~Genesis 50:20, NIV

■ **Today's Snapshot: The Bold Brothers**

In every situation Joseph faced, he never let go of his confidence in God. Over time, Joseph developed a tremendous amount of spiritual endurance. God blessed Joseph from the pit to the prison to the palace.

Joseph's brothers were jealous of the relationship he had with his father, so they wanted to kill him. God protected Joseph and gave them the opportunity to sell him into slavery instead. From the home where Joseph faithfully served as a slave, he ended up in prison. While in prison, Joseph interpreted a dream which eventually led him to be released to interpret the Pharoah's dreams. The Pharaoh respected Joseph so much because he was such a man of integrity. Joseph became Pharaoh's right-hand man! This prestigious position allowed Joseph to save food to prepare for the upcoming famine which hit Egypt and the surrounding nations hard. Joseph's brothers and their families were hungry. When they could no longer feed themselves, their hunger led them to Egypt where they could get food from Pharaoh's storehouses. Joseph recognized his brothers, reconciled with them, and they bowed down to him just as he pictured in his boyhood dream.

day three

God strategically planted Joseph in a place to preserve his family—the twelve tribes of Israel. Through the lineage of Joseph's brother Judah, the spiritual seed passes into the arms of the young mother, whose baby arrived to offer eternal reconciliation to the world.

> *Away in a manger, no crib for a bed*
>
> *The little Lord Jesus lay down His sweet head*
>
> *The stars in the sky look down where he lay*
>
> *The little Lord Jesus asleep in the hay.*
>
> *-Anonymous, (1884)*

■ **Family Discussion:**
- Do you have a favorite colorful coat? Can you describe it?
- Jealousy is common among siblings. Regarding your family members, what causes jealousy to stir in you?
- How do you build spiritual endurance to help you withstand trials?
  {pray, read the Bible, read a devotional, spend time in worship}

■ **Closing Prayer:**
Heavenly Father,
*We praise You for Your presence in every aspect of our lives. Sometimes it feels like we are in a pit and we need spiritual endurance. Thank You for reminding us that Your promises are eternal, regardless of the situations we face here on earth. Thank You for preparing our hearts in the good times so we are ready to face the difficult times. Thank You for the story of Joseph as we see You took him from the pit to the palace, by way of the prison. Your hand was on him the entire time. You knew exactly where You were taking him to preserve Your nation to bring forth Your Son. We praise You for the **big picture** which is Your strategic plan and is so much more than our human hearts and finite eyes can see. Thank You for this season and the reason to celebrate the birth of Your Son.*
In the precious name of Jesus we pray, Amen

THE STRATEGIC SISTER

The bond between sisters begins at birth. Even though I was only three, I remember the moment my parents brought home my baby sister from the hospital. To this day, regardless of how far apart my sister and I live, our bond remains steady. Throughout our lifetime, we have laughed, cried, and rejoiced as we journeyed through family events: holidays, divorces, engagements, marriages, birthdays, and babies.

Miles and miles of running bonded us together when we lived close enough to squeeze in weekend runs. I will always remember and treasure how she held my hand to pull me across the Disney Marathon finish line. We trained for the race together, and we promised each other we would finish together. When I hit the wall at twenty-four miles, with two miles left to go, she encouraged me, and she held my hand until the end. Today she continues to push me to be my best, and I am grateful.

Miriam wanted her brother to survive, so after her mother placed him in the basket, she watched him float right down the Nile river into the Pharaoh's palace. Pharaoh's daughter drew Moses out of the water and Miriam found the perfect woman to nurse the baby for her—their mother.

Photographer Wendy Sander

peace

day four

Moses grew up in the palace, but he killed an Egyptian who was mistreating a Hebrew, one of his own kind, and fled to Midian when held accountable.

In the wilderness, God met Moses face-to-face through a burning bush and God used Moses to deliver His people through a series of plagues which ended with the blood of an unblemished lamb.

■ **Today's Scripture:**

Then his sister asked Pharaoh's daughter, "Shall I go and get one of the Hebrew women to nurse the baby for you?" ~Exodus 2:7, NIV

*When the child grew older, she took him to Pharaoh's daughter and he became her son. She named him Moses, saying, "I drew him out of the water."
~Exodus 2:10, NIV*

*Moses said to God, "Suppose I go to the Israelites and say to them, 'The God of your fathers has sent me to you,' and they ask me, 'What is his name?' Then what shall I tell them?" God said to Moses, "I AM WHO I AM. This is what you are to say to the Israelites: 'I AM has sent me to you.' God also said to Moses, "Say to the Israelites, 'The Lord, the God of your fathers—the God of Abraham, the God of Isaac and the God of Jacob—has sent me to you.' This is my name forever, the name you shall call me from generation to generation."
~Exodus 3:13-15, NIV*

"…For I know the plans I have for you," declares the Lord, "plans to prosper you and not to harm you, plans to give you hope and a future…" ~Jeremiah 29:11, NIV

*By faith Moses, when he had grown up, refused to be known as the son of Pharaoh's daughter. He chose to be mistreated along with the people of God rather than to enjoy the fleeting pleasures of sin. He regarded disgrace for the sake of Christ as of greater value than the treasures of Egypt, because he was looking ahead to his reward. By faith he left Egypt, not fearing the king's anger; he persevered because he saw him who is invisible. By faith, he kept the Passover and the application of blood, so that the destroyer of the firstborn would not touch the firstborn of Israel. By faith the people passed through the Red Sea as on dry land; but when the Egyptians tried to do so, they were drowned.
~Hebrews 11:24-29 NIV*

■ Today's Snapshot: The Strategic Sister

The Israelites thrived under Joseph's leadership in Egypt. However, when Joseph died, the new Pharaoh condemned the brothers and their families to slavery. The Israelites quickly increased in size, and the new Pharaoh felt threatened. To weaken the Israelites, Pharaoh killed all the Hebrew baby boys by throwing them into the Nile. But by the grace of God, one Hebrew boy survived. The baby's basket floated out of bondage and straight into freedom.

Who would have known that a few years later this baby would lead the entire Hebrew nation out of bondage and straight into freedom?

God got his attention in a burning bush and told Moses that He was the God of the Patriarchs and He was going to deliver His people from their affliction and suffering. The one who was *delivered* would soon become the *deliverer*.

Moses returned to Egypt to beg Pharoah to let God's people go. When Pharoah refused, Moses guided the Hebrew people through ten plagues. During each plague, the Hebrews were protected while the Egyptians were affected. After God delivered the Israelites by the blood from the unblemished lamb, Miriam sang and praised God. Through her brother's life, Miriam saw God's fingerprints.

The life of Moses provided a way for joy to come to the world, one quiet night, in a manger over 2,000 years ago.

Joy to the world, the Lord is come!

Let earth receive her King;

Let every heart prepare Him room,

And heaven and nature sing,

And heaven and nature sing,

And heaven, and heaven, and nature sing.

~Isaac Watts (1674-1748)

■ **Family Discussion:**
- What's the best thing about your place in the family birth order?
- What is the worst thing about your place in the family birth order?

■ **Closing Prayer:**

Heavenly Father,

We praise You for sweet sisters and bonds which begin at birth. Regardless of the space between siblings, the bond is always there. Miriam looked out for her brother and encouraged him as the deliverer. She knew there was something special about that baby. We praise You for the deliverance of the Hebrew nation by the blood of the Lamb which allowed for the lineage to be preserved through the tribe of Judah. We praise You for this Christmas season as we anticipate the arrival of Your Son, who became our own sacrificial lamb. May we continue to prepare our homes and our hearts for His arrival.

In the precious name of Jesus we pray, Amen

A GUIDING FATHER-IN-LAW

Some fathers-in-law impact the family by their direct presence, and some impact the family by the legacy they leave behind.

My husband grew up on the continent of Africa. He lived in many different countries, but his favorite country was his beloved Tanzania. He shares wonderful stories of the beautiful people, carving markets, fish markets, swim records, and adventures on the Indian ocean with his father. They called him Bwana which in Swahili means "Boss."

While Bwana wasn't always present for his family, he worked hard to provide for them. I only knew him for a few years, because Bwana passed away early on in our marriage. At the time, my husband had just helped his father purchase a boat so that he could continue his love of boating and fishing while back in America. After Bwana passed away, my husband purchased Bwana's boat from my mother-in-law and named it *Bwana's Legacy*.

Even though my father-in-law has not been present, his legacy of hard work, determination, and love of being on the water was passed down to my husband, and continues to impact our family to this day. Jethro, Moses' father-in-law, gave Moses clear and consise advice on how to lead the Hebrew nation.

■ **Today's Scripture:**
El Elyon. God Most High. Psalm 7:17

> *Then Moses went out to meet his father-in-law, and he bowed down and kissed him; and they asked each other of their welfare and went into the tent. Moses told his father-in-law all that the LORD had done to Pharaoh and to the Egyptians for Israel's sake, all the hardship that had befallen them on the journey, and how the LORD had delivered them.*

peace

day five

Jethro rejoiced over all the goodness which the LORD had done to Israel, in delivering them from the hand of the Egyptians. Then Jethro, Moses' father-in-law, took a burnt offering and sacrifices for God, and Aaron came with all the elders of Israel to eat a meal with Moses' father-in-law before God.
~Exodus 18:7-9, 12

Now when Moses' father-in-law saw all that he was doing for the people, he said, "What is this thing that you are doing for the people? Why do you alone sit as judge and all the people stand about you from morning to evening?"

Moses said to his father-in-law, "Because the people come to me to inquire of God. When they have a dispute, it comes to me, and I judge between a man and his neighbor and make known the statutes of God and His laws."

Moses' father-in-law said to him, "The thing that you are doing is not good. You will surely wear out, both yourself and these people who are with you, for the task is too heavy for you; you cannot do it alone." ~Exodus 18:14-18

"... Furthermore, you shall select out of all the people able men who fear God, men of truth, those who hate dishonest gain; and you shall place these over them as leaders ... Let them judge the people at all times; and let it be that every major dispute they will bring to you, but every minor dispute they themselves will judge. So it will be easier for you, and they will bear the burden with you. If you do this thing and God so commands you, then you will be able to endure, and all these people also will go to their place in peace." So Moses listened to his father-in-law and did all that he had said. ~Exodus 18:21-24, selected

■ Today's Snapshot: A Guiding Father-in-Law

Moses and his father-in-law Jethro {the Priest of Midian} had a strong relationship. Jethro filled the shoes of the father Moses never had. Moses earned Jethro's respect, and Jethro supported Moses. Their relationship grew stronger as they spent time together in fellowship.

After Jethro praised God and rejoiced, he spent time with Moses and his family. During this time, Jethro became quite concerned for Moses. His burden was too heavy.

Each day, from sunup to sundown, Moses sat alone and judged the people. When there was a disagreement, the people took it to Moses, and he settled it.

Jethro told Moses that Moses could not handle all the disputes on his own. He needed to find other Godly men who did not desire selfish gain, train them in God's law, and let them help by judging the smaller disputes.

Moses needed to delegate some of the responsibility to other Godly leaders! They would bear the smaller burdens, and the larger disagreements should be brought to Moses' attention (Exodus 18).

Moses followed the wisdom of his father-in-law who loved him. Jethro's wisdom—and Moses' ability to humbly listen to him—impacted the great Hebrew nation and paved the way for the King of kings to come to this world.

■ **Family Discussion:**
- Who helps you make decisions in your family?
- Do you have a father-in-law in your family who has made an impact directly or indirectly? If so, how?

■ **Closing Prayer:**
Heavenly Father,
We praise You for Godly men whom You sent to impact a nation so many years ago. We thank You for the loving, honest relationship between Moses and Jethro. We praise You for the lesson of humility Moses demonstrated in his respect for his family elder, so much so that when Jethro extended wisdom and guidance, Moses gladly responded and the nation continued to thrive under Moses' leadership. Thank You for the wisdom of the elders in our families and churches, and the legacy of hard work and determination passed down in many families. Each and every day we are grateful for Your presence. Today, we are one day closer to celebrating the birth of the King of kings, born in the manger centuries ago. In the precious name of Jesus we pray, Amen

peace

A WISE LEADER

Every family has a leader to show the way, just as every flock has a shepherd. God created the family with the father as the leader, but in many families, the father is not present, so the mother or an older sibling takes the responsibility of leading the flock.

Good leaders establish expectations and boundaries to avoid chaos, keep the peace, and provide safety and protection. When boundaries are established in love, they are met with honor, and they are not burdensome. Expectations and boundaries allow for bonds of trust, respect, and accountability to form within the family.

On the top of Mt. Sinai, God delivered His commandments for those within His family, and through love, He gave them directly to the leader He placed within His people.

■ **Today's Scripture:**
The Ten Commandments (Exodus 20)

1. **You shall have no other gods before Me.**
2. **You shall not make idols.**
3. **You shall not take the name of the LORD your God in vain.**
4. **Remember the Sabbath day, to keep it holy.**
5. **Honor your father and mother.**
6. **You shall not murder.**
7. **You shall not commit adultery.**
8. **You shall not steal.**
9. **You shall not bear false witness against your neighbor.**
10. **You shall not covet.**

So He declared to you His covenant which He commanded you to perform, that is, the Ten Commandments; and He wrote them on two tablets of stone.
~Deuteronomy 4:13

day six

Hear, O Israel! The LORD is our God, the LORD is one! You shall love the LORD your God with all your heart and with all your soul and with all your might. These words, which I am commanding you today, shall be on your heart. You shall teach them diligently to your sons and shall talk of them when you sit in your house and when you walk by the way and when you lie down and when you rise up. ~Deuteronomy 6:4-7

"This is My commandment, that you love one another, just as I have loved you." ~John 15:12

In fact, this is love for God: to keep his commands. And his commands are not burdensome... ~1 John 5:3, NIV

Whatever you do, do your work heartily, as for the Lord rather than for men. ~Colossians 3:23

■ Today's Snapshot: A Wise Leader

God wrote His "family rules" on the top of Mt. Sinai with Moses while He was shaping the Israelites as a nation. God knew the nation needed guidance and boundaries, written by His hand through love. God wrote the commands with His finger on tablets of stone for His people (Exodus 31:18).

God's commands were set for our safety and protection.

These commands came as a result of His presence, for His purpose, to establish His peace. The Ten Commandments represent God's moral law. However, with Adam's sin nature within each of us, as hard as we try, we cannot keep them all.

We are imperfect people who serve a perfect God.

That's why God sent Jesus. By His blood, we move into the covenant of grace. However, we still adhere to God's moral law, because when true love exists in the heart, it also exists in the will. This Christmas season we celebrate the baby who came to offer our hearts grace, mercy, and forgiveness.

God gave Him to the world through love, and in love, He wraps His arms around us completely.

■ Family Discussion:
- What other rules does your family have that are not listed above?
- Which one family expectation is the hardest for you to keep? Why?
- Why is love the most important command?

■ Closing Prayer:
Heavenly Father,
We praise You for boundaries, expectations, and good leaders whom You have placed within our family to guide us. These commands—written with Your mighty finger from Your heart to the tablets of stone—display Your love to Your people. Help us to keep You first in every aspect of our lives as we love You with all of our hearts, minds, souls, and strength. When our hearts fully understand Your sacrificial love, true love is born and exists in our will. We live up to Your expectations not because we have to, but because we love You. Thank You for loving us completely by sending Your Son on that silent night so many years ago. In the precious name of Jesus we pray, Amen

Rejoice in the Lord always; again I say rejoice!

~Philippians 4:4

THIRD SUNDAY

Joy

Rejoice in the Lord always; again, I will say, rejoice! ~Philippians 4:4

There is a time for everything, and a season for every activity under the heavens. ~Ecclesiastes 3:1, NIV

When God tells us to rejoice He does not mean for us to have joy regarding the situation we are facing, but rather to remember that we have JOY because of the Savior who was born to die, rise again, and live as our everyday hope!

The virgin will conceive and give birth to a son, and they will call him Immanuel (which means "God with us"). ~Matthew 1:23, NIV

This third Sunday of Advent, we light a candle for joy.

The baby Jesus was born to die so that we may live. Jesus conquered death by rising again to be with the Father and in Him we will overcome as well! In Christ, we will live forever with those whom we love because He came for us.

When Jesus physically left this world, He gave us the gift of His Presence in the Holy Spirit. Immanuel means *God with us*. Joy has come into the world right into our hurting hearts. We have Joy in Christ because we have victory in Him over all circumstances. In the good and the not-so-good, God is with us. He overcame, and in Him, so will we, one day.

We rejoice in knowing He came for us! He is with us! And He will come again!
This is a season of rejoicing!

May the eyes of our hearts be opened to see the *big picture* and experience the joy which comes from having a fresh perspective! God with us ~ Immanuel!

O come, O come, Emmanuel

And ransom captive Israel

That mourns in lonely exile here

Until the Son of God appears

Rejoice! Rejoice! Emmanuel

Shall come to thee, O Israel.

O come, Thou Rod of Jesse, free

Thine own from Satan's tyranny

From depths of Hell Thy people save

And give them victory o'er the grave

Rejoice! Rejoice! Emmanuel

Shall come to thee, O Israel.

O come, Thou Dayspring, come and cheer

Our spirits by Thine advent here

Disperse the gloomy clouds of night

And death's dark shadows put to flight.

Rejoice! Rejoice! Emmanuel

Shall come to thee, O Israel.

~Thomas Helmore (1851)

The heavens declare the glory of God, and the sky above proclaims his handiwork.
~Psalm 19:1, ESV

Joy to the world, the Lord is come!

Let earth receive her King!

Let every heart prepare Him room.

And heaven and nature sing!

And heaven and nature sing!

And heaven and nature sing!

    -Isaac Watts (1674-1748)

And when the indescribable JOY enters your heart it is called *naches*.

May your hearts be filled with an abundance of peace and everlasting JOY.
Now is the time to rejoice!

Rejoice, the King has come and He lives in us!

Happy Sunday!

A COMPASSIONATE TEACHER

We all have that favorite teacher or coach who stretched us further than we ever thought we could go and helped us to achieve more than we ever imagined we could reach.

Looking back over the years allows us to see how God used these special people to impact our lives and shape us into who we are today. On the first day of school, I was scared to death of my fifth-grade teacher. All of my friends had the *other* teacher, and I begged my mom to switch me to her classroom. In my mind, if she didn't do it, I could not go back to school! She made me go—every day. That year turned out to be my favorite year in grade school. That experience taught me to trust my mom who could see the *big picture*. My teacher impacted my life in more ways than he will ever know.

I can also name coaches who invested their time in me to help me become who I am today.

Good teachers partner with parents to impart wisdom and help *raise up* children in the way they should go.

I had another teacher, whose love, guidance, and wisdom in the Word led me to the heart of God. She taught me that He knew me, and she taught me how to find Him to know Him. She taught me how to read God's Word, study God's Word, and begin to understand God's Word, which changed my life and my heart forever. Her instruction and Godly wisdom impacted my life, so that I may impact others for Him.

Moses taught Joshua and mentored him as Joshua became the next leader of the Hebrew nation.

■ **Today's Scripture:**
Now Joshua the son of Nun was filled with the spirit of wisdom, for Moses had laid his hands on him, and the sons of Israel listened to him and did as the Lord had commanded Moses. ~Deuteronomy 34:9

I will instruct you and teach you in the way you should go;
I will counsel you with my loving eye on you. ~Psalm 32:8, NIV

"No one will be able to stand against you all the days of your life. As I was with Moses, so I will be with you; I will never leave you nor forsake you. Be strong and courageous, because you will lead these people to inherit the land I swore to their ancestors to give them.

Be strong and very courageous. Be careful to obey all the law my servant Moses gave you; do not turn from it to the right or to the left, that you may be successful wherever you go." ~Joshua 1:5-7, NIV

■ **Today's Snapshot: A Compassionate Teacher**
Moses imparted Godly wisdom to Joshua. Moses taught Joshua how to know God, listen to God, and follow God. He helped Joshua understand God's heart so he could lead God's people to fulfill God's purpose in the *big picture*.

day one

Moses was a great teacher. As a result, Joshua followed God and led the twelve tribes of Israel into freedom, which continued to light the way for the coming of the King.

■ **Family Discussion:**
- Who was your favorite teacher or coach? What made him/her so special?
- How will you impact others as your teacher/coach impacted you?
- Do you have a specific person who led you to the heart of God, or in other words, helped you find Jesus?

■ **Closing Prayer:**

Heavenly Father,

*We praise You for the wisdom you passed down from Moses to Joshua, and for the words You gave directly to him. We praise You for the people whom You have placed in our lives as teachers and coaches. We are better people because of them, and our family has benefited greatly. I praise You for the people in our lives who taught us about You and brought us to You. Please help us continue to spend time in Your Word—not straying to the right or the left by worldly distractions. May this Christmas season be different from all others, as we celebrate Your Son and see His role in the **big picture**.*

In the precious name of Jesus we pray, Amen

A DEVOTED MOTHER-IN-LAW

Over Christmas a few years ago, my mother-in-law took our family to Africa so the children could see where their father grew up. For almost two weeks we traveled the country, experienced the culture, and served in the beautiful country of Tanzania. She blessed us with this opportunity so that we would know. In order to know, we had to experience it. In that short time, we had a glimpse into the culture, the people, and into my husband's childhood. From the swimming pool where he held the fastest freestyle record to the gated and guarded homes he grew up in...from hiking up to Mt. Kilimanjaro's first base camp to waking up Christmas morning in the middle of the Serengeti—we got a taste of what he experienced as a child.

The people and places that he loves made their way into our hearts, too.

day two

My heart swelled with gratitude upon our arrival at the Tumani Home of Widows and Orphans. In Swahili *tumani* means hope. The orphaned children were praising God in Swahili, and our hearts were praising Him, too—two different languages, yet united as one in the Spirit. We thanked God for the opportunity to visit and to serve, and for the fresh perspective which He provided through my mother-in-law.

When Ruth married into Naomi's family, God redeemed her and gave her a fresh perspective on love and life. Ruth embraced her fresh perspective and as a result, her redemption story is perfectly placed into the lineage of the King of kings.

■ Today's Scripture:

But Ruth said, "Do not urge me to leave you or turn back from following you; for where you go, I will go, and where you lodge, I will lodge. Your people shall be my people, and your God, my God." ~Ruth 1:16

"May the LORD reward your work, and your wages be full from the LORD, the God of Israel, under whose wings you have come to seek refuge." ~Ruth 2:12

So Boaz took Ruth and she became his wife, … and she gave birth to a son.... Then Naomi took the child in her arms and cared for him. The women living there said, "Naomi has a son!" And they named him Obed. He was the father of Jesse, the father of David. ~Ruth 4:13, 16-17, NIV

■ Today's Snapshot: A Devoted Mother-in-law

Naomi and Ruth had a beautiful relationship. Ruth loved her mother-in-law and her mother-in-law loved her. When Ruth's husband passed away, she should have returned to her family in her country; however, she faithfully remained with Naomi because through Naomi's family, Ruth found God. God knew Ruth's heart and her new perspective. He knew how much she loved Him. As a result, God wove Ruth into His *big picture*.

After Ruth lost her husband, she had the desire to marry again, so Naomi searched for a kinsman redeemer. A kinsman redeemer is a family member who could redeem, or buy back, what was lost.

Ruth gleaned wheat on a field where a man named Boaz worked. When Ruth told Naomi she had worked with Boaz, Naomi was overjoyed! Boaz was a distant relative who could be her kinsman redeemer.

Naomi sent Ruth to the wheat threshing floor to make her identity known to him, and Boaz fell in love with Ruth, partly because of her loyalty and faithfulness to her family.

Ruth's faithfulness to the God of her mother-in-law shined the light for love to travel through a Moabite woman to the lineage of a tremendous Israelite king, down to the manger 2,000 years later.

The spiritual lineage is passed

from Adam,

    to Noah,

        to Abraham,

            to Isaac,

                to Jacob (whose name we know as Israel),

                    to Moses,

                        to Joshua,

                            to Obed (Ruths's son),

                          to Jesse,

                      to David,

                      to Isaiah,

                              ...and eventually through the young girl, Mary,
                                        to the baby Jesus, to you.

■ **Family Discussion:**
- Think about your ancestors. Which one would you like to meet?
- Explain why this ancestor is so important to you.

■ **Closing Prayer:**

Heavenly Father,

We praise You for the perfect picture of faithfulness displayed by Ruth to Naomi. You use people whom we would least expect to carry out Your plan. Ruth's faithfulness to her mother-in-law sets a beautiful example for all to follow. We praise You for the redemption story displayed through Ruth's story. As we seek You may we continue to set our eyes on the birth of one perfect, precious baby this Christmas season. Thank You for sending Your Son who is the beautiful picture of redemption for each one of us.

In the precious name of Jesus we pray, Amen

A HIDDEN HERITAGE

When I think of my sister's or brother's children, I think of them as my own. I love them as my own, I adore them as my own, and I pray for them as if they were my own children. I even pray for many of my students as I pray for my own children!

I am never surprised when I see God move through the lives of young people.

Sometimes it takes a special person to help our youth recognize how He places ordinary people where He wants to use them in extraordinary ways. The lineage of the coming King continued to travel through God's chosen people when God planned for the Persian king to marry a young Jewish girl named Esther. God strategically placed Esther and her hidden heritage in a position of influence for His perfect plan to prevail.

day three

The story of Esther helps us to see the ties that bind extended family members. In the context of family, it is obvious that Mordecai loved Esther as his own child. And Esther found favor with all who knew her.

■ Today's Scripture:

Now when the turn of Esther, the daughter of Abihail the uncle of Mordecai who had taken her as his daughter, came to go into the king, she did not request anything except what Hegai, the king's eunuch who was in charge of the women, advised. And Esther found favor in the eyes of all who saw her.
~Esther 2:15

But Esther had kept secret her family background and nationality just as Mordecai had told her to do, for she continued to follow Mordecai's instructions as she had done when he was bringing her up.
~Esther 2:20, NIV

Let no one look down on your youthfulness, but rather in speech, conduct, love, faith and purity, show yourself an example of those who believe.
~1 Timothy 4:12

■ Today's Snapshot: A Hidden Heritage

We stomped our feet loudly and shook the noisemakers fiercely when the Rabbi read Haman's name from the Scriptures during the annual Purim celebration. As a young girl, I clearly remember hearing the story of Esther read aloud at the synagogue.

As we take a look at the *big picture*, it becomes clear that God does not use obvious people to carry out his plans. His ways are better and higher than ours and His purpose is sometimes easier to see when we look backward in time. Hindsight is 20/20, as they say.

King Xerses, arrogantly dismissed his first wife, Vashti, from the royal throne and chose a young Jewish girl named Esther to fill her shoes. The king did not know of Esther's Jewish heritage when she was picked out of the many beautiful women to become his new queen.

When the Hebrew nation was threatened to be destroyed by Haman's evil plan, Esther's royal position allowed for her to be in the perfect place at the perfect time to carry out God's purpose for His chosen people. Only the king's wife could change the king's heart in one pivotal moment of time.

Esther's placement in the Persian palace allowed for the entire Hebrew nation to be perfectly preserved and for God to send a baby through them in His perfect timing to a broken and hurting world that needed a Savior.

■ **Family Discussion:**
- How do you think Esther felt when she found out the king chose her to be his queen? Do you think she realized how important her role would be?
- If you look backward on your own story, can you see moments where God has preserved you for "such a time as this?"

Isn't it awesome to witness how much work God does behind the scenes to prepare the way for the birth of the newborn King? Joy to the world! The Lord is come! Let earth receive her King!!

■ **Closing Prayer:**
Heavenly Father,
We love looking back to see Your fingerprints on the lives of the specific people in the lineage of Jesus Christ all the way forward to the people in our lives whom You strategically placed to individually lead us to Christ. Thank You for the gift of sight to see the Light as it was preserved through God's chosen people and traveled to Mary's arms and into our hearts.
In the precious name of Jesus we pray, Amen

AN ADORING AUNT

Families travel from near and far to celebrate the holidays together. A sense of oneness is found when siblings, parents, grandparents, aunts, uncles, and cousins gather, and a deep longing is present when certain family members are missing. There is a special comfort found in being with those who love you and know you best.

My daughter adores her Aunt Rooney. Rooney is fashionable and fun, yet similar in a comforting way to her mom because she is her sister. There is no doubt that a special relationship exists between an aunt and a niece or nephew.

Mary traveled to visit her relative Elizabeth and a rush of excitement filled the air. Each woman was at a completely different age and stage of life.

The perfect time to have a first child is unique for everyone—especially when God is in the process of working miracles through the parents. Elizabeth in her old age became pregnant, and Mary conceived the Hope of the world!

■ **Today's Scripture:**
The angel replied, "The Holy Spirit will come upon you, and the power of the Most High will overshadow you. So the baby to be born will be holy, and he will be called the Son of God. What's more, your relative Elizabeth has become pregnant in her old age! People used to say she was barren, but she has conceived a son and is now in her sixth month. For nothing is impossible with God."
Mary responded, "I am the Lord's servant. May everything you have said about me come true." And then the angel left her.
A few days later Mary hurried to the hill country of Judea, to the town where Zechariah lived. She entered the house and greeted Elizabeth. At the sound of Mary's greeting, Elizabeth's child leaped within her, and Elizabeth was filled with the Holy Spirit.
Elizabeth gave a glad cry and exclaimed to Mary, "God has blessed you above all women, and your child is blessed. Why am I so honored, that the mother of my Lord should visit me? When I heard your greeting, the baby in my womb jumped for joy. You are blessed because you believed that the Lord would do what he said." ~Luke 1:35-45, NLT

But Jesus looked at them and said, "With man this is impossible, but with God all things are possible." ~Matthew 19:26, ESV

■ Today's Snapshot: An Adoring Aunt

Mary trusted the Lord, but she needed a comfortable place to mentally process the promise found growing within her. Elizabeth's home was a safe place for her heavy heart to land.

As soon as Elizabeth saw Mary, Elizabeth's baby jumped with joy. Elizabeth confirmed to Mary what her heart already knew.

Even though it appeared physically impossible, Mary was carrying the Son of God, because *nothing is impossible for God*.

God blessed Mary because she believed. Mary believed and she became the mother of the baby who would reconcile the world.

75

day four

■ Family Discussion:

- If you were able to live with an extended family member for a year, whom would you choose? Why?
- Mary was faithful. She believed, and God blessed her. Is it easy or hard for you to believe the Christmas story?

■ Closing Prayer:

Heavenly Father,

We praise You for our families. Those who live with us, those who live afar, and those friends whom we consider family. We praise You for the gift of time that You give us over the holidays to reconnect with our loved ones. May we use the gift of time to rest and celebrate our love for You. We praise You for Mary's belief. She believed You, and You worked a miracle through her. Like Mary, may our hearts believe in the miracle which took place when You sent Your son to the manger and gave joy to the world.

In the precious name of Jesus we pray, Amen

joy

THE SIGNIFICANT STEP-FATHER

Most young men envision getting married, finding a good job, and starting families of their own one day. In their youth, they usually don't begin by saying, "I want to be a stepfather."

The role of a stepfather is often under appreciated and can be rather difficult. However, as God's will unfolds, many children are blessed to have certain men assume this great responsibility by taking on this important position in the family.

Joseph, betrothed and at first glance betrayed by Mary, stepped up to the plate when the opportunity presented itself to him. When Joseph found out Mary was pregnant, he secretly planned to send her away, until he understood that His purpose was much larger than he ever could have imagined.

day five

■ **Today's Scripture:**

The angel answered and said to him, "I am Gabriel, who stands in the presence of God, and I have been sent to speak to you and to bring you this good news." ~Luke 1:19

… "Joseph, son of David, do not be afraid to take Mary as your wife; for the Child who has been conceived in her is of the Holy Spirit. She will bear a Son; and you shall call His name Jesus, for He will save His people from their sins." ~Matthew 1:20b-21

■ **Today's Snapshot: The Significant Step-Father**

Suddenly, Joseph's troubled heart became quiet and calm. His doubt shifted to belief. Mary was chosen to give birth to the Son of God, and since Mary was promised to him, he began to understand that they were chosen to raise the Son of God together. What an honor!

It wasn't the direction Joseph was anticipating. However, hope soon replaced fear, and Joseph walked confidently in his God-given role. Joseph became the stepfather to the baby who brought peace and redemption to the hurting world.

The Son, whom Joseph was chosen to raise, is celebrated as the Prince of Peace and King of kings.

■ **Family Discussion:**
• Has God ever changed your direction in life?
• Was it easy or difficult for you to change directions?
• What if Joseph had not been obedient to the direction God was telling him to go?

■ **Closing Prayer:**

Heavenly Father,
We praise You for Your sovereignty and for Joseph's obedient heart. By willingly following You, in spite of society's opposition, he set an example for us all. May we spend time daily in Your Word getting to know You, so that when a change comes we will follow in the direction You want us to go. Tonight, may we sleep in heavenly peace as we anticipate the birth of Your Son!
In the precious name of Jesus we pray, Amen

THE DEDICATED MOTHER

The bowl flew out of my hand and smashed into a million pieces on my kitchen floor. My full hands missed the grip completely. When I knelt to pick up the pieces, the story of my life flashed before my eyes. Whole at the beginning of time, then broken and separated from oneness, goodness, and truth, only to be joyfully reconciled through one tiny baby. Through the ancestors in my faith family-tree, our Father picked up the pieces of my broken life and carefully, yet tenderly, put them back together in His perfect way.

**When it looks as if our lives are falling to pieces,
God takes brokenness and restores it to beauty.**

day six

It's not a beauty equal to what the world considers beautiful, but it is a beauty that radiates from within as a result of a heart understanding of His restoration when He meets us right where we are in our mess. God's immense love radiates from within when we understand we are complete in Him because we are His masterpiece, and we are a snapshot in His *big picture*. Our lives matter—even the tiniest details are important to Him—because He is working through each of us in our parts of the world to fulfill His master plan.

God revealed Himself, after 400 years of silence, to the heart of one girl who became one young mother. For a moment it looked as if her world was falling apart until she understood she was the one chosen to birth the baby who would bring reconciliation to the world. God keeps His promises.

■ **Today's Scripture:**

A shoot will come up from the stump of Jesse; from his roots a branch will bear fruit. ~Isaiah 11:1, NIV

For a child will be born to us, a son will be given to us; And the government will rest on His shoulders; And His name will be called Wonderful Counselor, Mighty God, Eternal Father, Prince of Peace. ~Isaiah 9:6

And coming in, he said to her, "Greetings, favored one! The Lord is with you." But she was very perplexed at this statement, and kept pondering what kind of salutation this was. The angel said to her, "Do not be afraid, Mary, for you have found favor with God. And behold, you will conceive in your womb and bear a son, and you shall name Him Jesus. He will be great and will be called the Son of the Most High; and the Lord God will give Him the throne of His father David; and He will reign over the house of Jacob forever, and His kingdom will have no end." ~Luke 1:28-33

■ **Today's Snapshot: The Dedicated Mother**

God used the willing condition of a young girl's heart to bring the Savior to the world through the lineage that grew right out of the Jesse tree. Mary was confused and perplexed, yet the angel Gabriel told her she had found favor with God. For a moment, it appeared as though her world had fallen to pieces.

One faithful heart was chosen to fulfill one promise to the world.

She could choose to trust the angel when he said, "Do not be afraid," or concede to her doubt and turn away from what he was asking her to do.

God chose Mary, not for her role in society, or for her years of wisdom, but rather for her willing, obedient, and faithful heart. Then she held her son for the first time. She felt his sweet skin on her damp chest and at that moment, the brokenness of the world collided with the promise of the Prince of Peace.

■ **Family Discussion:**
- In your life, where you are right now—student, mom, dad, friend—has God given you a responsibility? Remember, He often gives small responsibilities before He gives large ones. We can choose to trust Him and follow through, or we can choose to turn away.
- What are you doing today that will make an impact for Him tomorrow? Did you give someone a hug, show someone appreciation, or share the Christmas story?

■ **Closing Prayer:**
Heavenly Father,
We praise You for Mary's young, faithful, and obedient heart toward You and Your Word. Her life shows us how important it is to be responsible for the little things so that when You ask us to do something big, our hearts are ready. Even when it looked like her world was falling apart, and her heart did not understand the impact she would have on the world, she knew You, trusted You, and followed You. Thank You for her faithful example. Thank You for putting the pieces back together perfectly. We are eternally grateful and we continue to be amazed by the wonder of Your love.
In the precious name of Jesus we pray, Amen

FOURTH SUNDAY

Love

For God so loved the world that he gave his one and only Son,
that whoever believes in him shall not perish but have eternal life.
~John 3:16, NIV

If mankind had not sinned and broken God's heart in the beginning to cause an eternal separation, we would not need a Savior to bring us back to Him with love.

However, when the choice was made, God promised that the separation would not be forever. In the very beginning, God shared His redemption plan.

God promised that Someone would come in the future to crush the serpent's head and destroy evil, but the serpent would bruise Him first.

And I will put enmity between you and the woman, and between your offspring and hers; he will crush your head, and you will strike his heel. ~Genesis 3:15, NIV

On the fourth Sunday of Advent, we light the candle for **LOVE**.

I will declare that your love stands firm forever, that you have established your faithfulness in heaven itself. You said, "I have made a covenant with my chosen one, I have sworn to David my servant, 'I will establish your line forever and make your throne firm through all generations.' "
~Psalm 89:2-4, NIV

"Therefore the Lord Himself will give you a sign: Behold, a virgin will be with child and bear a son, and will call His name Immanuel." ~Isaiah 7:14, NIV

The angel went to her and said, "Greetings, you who are highly favored! The Lord is with you." Mary was greatly troubled at his words and wondered what kind of greeting this might be. But the angel said to her, "Do not be afraid, Mary; you have found favor with God." ~Luke 1:28-30, NIV

The angel Gabriel, whose name itself means strength, gave Mary strength for the journey which lay ahead of her.

Hope, peace, and joy were born out of the greatest gift of love.

Mary's baby came through the lineage of Abraham, Judah, and David, just as the prophets foretold. This love came from the Father, through a mother, into a baby for the world and straight into our hearts.

For this reason also, God highly exalted Him, and bestowed on Him the name which is above every name, so that at the name of Jesus every knee will bow, of those who are in heaven and on earth and under the earth, and that every tongue will confess that Jesus Christ is Lord, to the glory of God the Father. ~Philippians 2:9-11

The prophets foretold the baby's arrival.

The baby came to reconcile mankind to the heart of God.

In love, God sent a baby one silent night to teach us how to live, to give us hope, to fill us with peace, to give us the gift of joy, and to bring us back to Himself.

God loved us first ...

We love, because He first loved us ~1 John 4:19

... so that we could love others.

Happy Sunday!

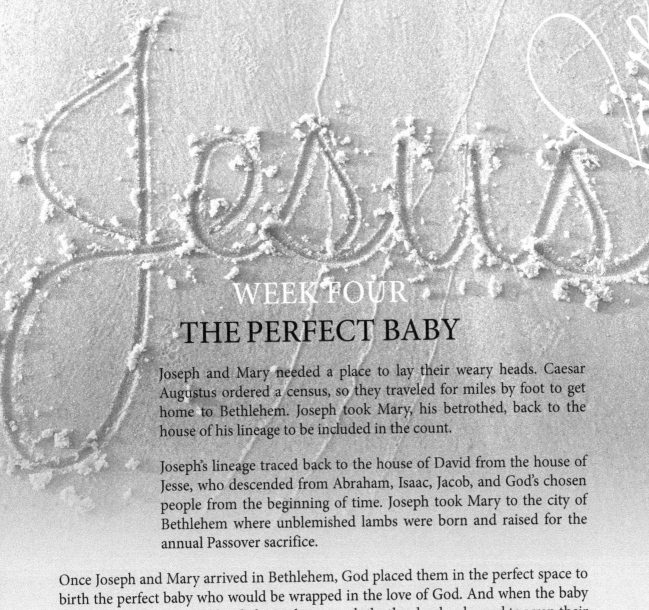

WEEK FOUR
THE PERFECT BABY

Joseph and Mary needed a place to lay their weary heads. Caesar Augustus ordered a census, so they traveled for miles by foot to get home to Bethlehem. Joseph took Mary, his betrothed, back to the house of his lineage to be included in the count.

Joseph's lineage traced back to the house of David from the house of Jesse, who descended from Abraham, Isaac, Jacob, and God's chosen people from the beginning of time. Joseph took Mary to the city of Bethlehem where unblemished lambs were born and raised for the annual Passover sacrifice.

Once Joseph and Mary arrived in Bethlehem, God placed them in the perfect space to birth the perfect baby who would be wrapped in the love of God. And when the baby was born, Mary wrapped her baby in the same cloths the shepherds used to wrap their perfect, unblemished, spotless lambs.[6]

Many followed the star to celebrate the birth of the Savior and worship the baby. It was the moment they had anticipated since the beginning of time!

As we place the star on the Christmas tree, the sound of Christmas carols mixed with the sweet smell of cinnamon rolls means it must be the morning we have anticipated. It's Christmas! There is a birthday in the house and it's time to celebrate! Break out the streamers, the balloons, and the cake! Bring out the gifts!

The angels proclaim, Jesus Christ is born! Glory to God! Peace on Earth!
The King of kings and Prince of Peace has arrived as a sweet baby and today the world takes time to pause, remember, and reflect upon the present of His earthly presence.

■ **Today's Scripture:**

"She will bear a Son; and you shall call His name Jesus, for He will save His people from their sins." ~Matthew 1:21

"Look! The virgin will conceive a child! She will give birth to a son, and they will call him Immanuel, which means 'God is with us.' " ~Matthew1:23, NLT

And while they were there, the time came for her baby to be born. She gave birth to her first child, a son. She wrapped him snugly in strips of cloth and laid him in a manger, because there was no lodging available for them. ~Luke 2:6-7, NLT

So the Word became human and made his home among us. He was full of unfailing love and faithfulness. And we have seen his glory, the glory of the Father's one and only Son. ~John 1:14, NLT

That night there were shepherds staying in the fields nearby, guarding their flocks of sheep. Suddenly, an angel of the Lord appeared among them, and the radiance of the Lord's glory surrounded them. They were terrified, but the angel reassured them. "Don't be afraid!" he said. "I bring you good news that will bring great joy to all people. The Savior—yes, the Messiah, the Lord—has been born today in Bethlehem, the city of David! And you will recognize him by this sign: You will find a baby wrapped snugly in strips of cloth, lying in a manger." Suddenly, the angel was joined by a vast host of others—the armies of heaven—praising God and saying, "Glory to God in highest heaven, and peace on earth to those with whom God is pleased."

When the angels had returned to heaven, the shepherds said to each other, "Let's go to Bethlehem! Let's see this thing that has happened, which the Lord has told us about."

They hurried to the village and found Mary and Joseph. And there was the baby, lying in the manger. After seeing him, the shepherds told everyone what had happened and what the angel had said to them about this child. All who heard the shepherds' story were astonished, but Mary kept all these things in her heart and thought about them often. The shepherds went back to their flocks, glorifying and praising God for all they had heard and seen. It was just as the angel had told them. ~Luke 2: 8-20, NLT

■ Today's Snapshot: The Perfect Baby

Jesus didn't come to our world as a mighty warrior but as the Prince of Peace. He wasn't born in a regal palace, yet He was considered the King of kings. The Jewish people were looking for someone to save them physically, but Jesus came to reconcile us to God and save us spiritually. The Perfect Baby descended from heaven to fill the gap which had been present in mankind since Adam and Eve chose to separate themselves from God. Gods plan all along was for the Perfect Baby to become the ultimate sacrifice.

Jesus came in love.
Jesus was love.

He came to show us how to live as the Father intended—with love.

Then, Jesus became the final sacrifice to atone for each of our sins, offer forgiveness, and offer eternal life to those who choose to believe.

God gave us the perfect gift in His Son.

The present is His presence {Immanuel} God with us until the very end.

Today we celebrate His birth and we look forward to His return!

■ **Family Discussion:**

• This Christmas, will you allow Him to open your heart, so that He may reveal His presence to you?

The promise is for all of us.

**When you accept the gift of His Son,
His PRESENCE fills you,
and you are grafted into the faith-family tree.**

■ **Closing Prayer:**

Heavenly Father,
*We praise You for the present of Your presence which is greater than any gift under the tree. Your Son is the greatest gift. May You open the eyes of our hearts, so that we are able to see how our stories are a snapshot of Your **big picture**. We know there is much more to come, because what we can see is only a glimpse of Your glory. Jesus is the Light of the world who came to our world because of the vast darkness. Today we are basking in Your Light. And the fullness of the presence of Christ in us {Immanuel} is radiating from within.*
Merry Christmas!

In the precious name of Jesus we pray, Amen

love

THE FORETELLING COUSIN

Down at the beach, a spectacular sunrise meets my eyes. On the horizon, pink, orange, and yellow hues cast across the sky, and it is as if God is presently painting with various brushstrokes on a wide-open blank canvas. The sheer beauty of the brilliant sky lights up the shore each morning and stuns me every time.

But the past few mornings I have noticed the shadows. They are not there until the water comes. After the waves break and as the water recedes, a beautiful reflection of the quiet sunrise observers appears in the shallow pool. The shadow of the reality of the people does not last long. It is elusive. However, when it is there, it is beautiful.

The shadow points the observer to the substance of the reality.

day two

John the Baptist brought a glimpse of what he knew his cousin would fulfill. John was a mere shadow of the reality that was to come.

■ **Today's Scripture:**

In the beginning was the Word, and the Word was with God, and the Word was God. He was at the beginning with God. All things came into being through Him, and apart from Him, nothing came into being that has come into being. In Him was life, and the life was the Light of men. The Light shines in the darkness, and the darkness did not comprehend it.

There came a man sent from God, whose name was John. He came as a witness, to testify about the Light so that all might believe through him. He was not the Light, but he came to testify about the Light.

There was the true Light which, coming into the world, enlightens every man. He was in the world, and the world was made through Him, and the world did not know Him. He came to His own, and those who were His own did not receive Him. But as many as received Him, to them He gave the right to become children of God, even to those who believe in His name, who were born, not of blood nor of the will of the flesh nor of the will of man, but of God. ~John 1:1-13

...things which are a mere shadow of what is to come; but the substance belongs to Christ. ~Colossians 2:17

The law is only a shadow of the good things that are coming—not the realities themselves. For this reason, it can never, by the same sacrifices repeated endlessly year after year, make perfect those who draw near to worship.
~Hebrews 10:1, NIV

■ **Today's Snapshot: The Foretelling Cousin**
John grew up in a Jewish home, so he would have studied the Scriptures and understood the foreshadowing of the coming Christ revealed there.

* Jesus is the offspring of the woman (Genesis 3:15).
* All nations and generations to come are blessed through Him (Genesis 26:4).

- Jesus is the Lamb of God (Exodus 12; Revelation 5:12).
- Jesus suffers as a result of others' actions (Genesis 50:12).
- Jesus is the Rock that provides everlasting water (1 Corinthians 10:3-4).

There was a beautiful shadow from the beginning of time whose source was the body of Christ. And everything we see today leads up to the reality of His return (Hebrews 9:28, Matthew 24:44).

John the Baptist loved his cousin. He clearly stated that he came only as a witness to testify about the Light who was to come.

■ **Family Discussion:**
- Describe your favorite cousin. What do you love about him or her?
- Have you reached out to him or her lately? What words could you send today to encourage him or her?

■ **Closing Prayer:**
Heavenly Father,
We praise You for Your presence in the shadow. We especially praise You for the gift of cousins. Cousins are so similar and so special. Which is why it must have been such a treat for John the Baptist to introduce his very own cousin! How special and what delight God must have felt when His very own Son was introduced to the world. We praise You for the gift of Your Son, who was the source of the shadow and the perfect cousin to John the Baptist. We place our focus today beyond the shadow, and in You we rest until Your great return!
In the precious name of Jesus we pray, Amen

THE CHOSEN BROTHERS

There is a creek across the street from my home that slowly snakes its way through the Lowcountry of South Carolina. Paddleboarding in the creek is one of my favorite family pastimes. We usually head out against the current of the creek and when we are finished with our journey we enjoy a beautiful float back to the dock.

So, when my son, Hunter, said, "Hurry, quick! I found something really cool you have to see! Follow me!" We rushed to the spot to see a school of redfish! The school was huge and so much fun to watch as the redfish swam together right underneath us!

Hunter paddled home quickly to retrieve his fishing pole and the next thing I knew he was catching our dinner! He cast his line, hooked a redfish, jumped ashore to reel it in, and then he strapped it down on the paddleboard to bring it home. I loved that delicious, fresh fish dinner and the sweet memory of his fun discovery.

When our hearts get excited about finding a treasure, we can't help but want to share it with others!

The Bible introduces ordinary people chosen to complete extraordinary tasks. Each disciple was an ordinary person, just like you and me. A few were brothers. One was a tax collector. God chose them so He could work through them by the power of the Holy Spirit.

■ **Today's Scripture:**
Again the next day John was standing with two of his disciples, and he looked at Jesus as He walked, and said, "Behold, the Lamb of God!" The two disciples heard him speak, and they followed Jesus. And Jesus turned and saw them following, and said to them, "What do you seek?" They said to Him, "Rabbi (which translated means Teacher), where are You staying?" He said to them, "Come, and you will see." So they came and saw where He was staying; and they stayed with Him that day, for it was about the tenth hour.

day three

One of the two who heard John speak and followed Him, was Andrew, Simon Peter's brother. He found first his own brother Simon and said to him, "We have found the Messiah" (which translated means Christ). He brought him to Jesus. Jesus looked at him and said, "You are Simon the son of John; you shall be called Cephas" (which is translated, Peter). The next day He purposed to go into Galilee, and He found Philip. And Jesus said to him, "Follow Me."

Now Philip was from Bethsaida, of the city of Andrew and Peter. Philip found Nathanael and said to him, "We have found Him of whom Moses in the Law and also the Prophets wrote—Jesus of Nazareth, the son of Joseph." Nathanael said to him, "Can any good thing come out of Nazareth?" Philip said to him, "Come and see."

Jesus saw Nathanael coming to Him, and said of him, "Behold, an Israelite indeed, in whom there is no deceit!" Nathanael said to Him, "How do You know me?" Jesus answered and said to him, "Before Philip called you, when you were under the fig tree, I saw you." Nathanael answered Him, "Rabbi, You are the Son of God; You are the King of Israel." Jesus answered and said to him, "Because I said to you that I saw you under the fig tree, do you believe? You will see greater things than these." And He said to him, "Truly, truly, I say to you, you will see the heavens opened and the angels of God ascending and descending on the Son of Man." ~John 1:35-51

■ Today's Snapshot: The Chosen Brothers

Even before God chose the disciples, He saw them. God saw Nathanael in his quiet time under the fig tree. He understood Nathanael's heart before God appeared to him and said, "Follow Me." Nathanael didn't have life all figured out, but Nathanael knew that life was found in the Word. His knowledge of the Word grew as a result of His love for God. Nathanael spent time with God and was able to recognize the Messiah for who He was when He came.

God sees you.
God sees your heart.
God asks you to do one thing.

Follow Me! ~John 1:43

God chose each of the disciples not for excellence in their career fields, but rather their pure and righteous hearts towards Him. God saw their hearts and reached out to each disciple to bring him close to Himself—to Jesus—to walk with the Word and to go one way.

Follow Me! ~John 1:43

God knows your heart. God sees your heart's intentions. He doesn't need you to be the best one on the team or the funniest one in the classroom. He doesn't need you to be *the* man at work or the most beautiful person on social media. All He asks is that we spend time in the Word so that we can understand the direction He wants us to go and recognize Him.

Follow Me! ~John 1:43

■ Family Discussion:
- What is something you once saw that was really exciting and you couldn't wait to share what you had seen?
- Nathanael spent time with God under the fig tree? When is your "fig tree" time? If you don't have a special time, when should that time be for you?

■ Closing Prayer:
Heavenly Father,
We praise You for the men whom have chosen to follow. You saw Nathaniel in his quiet time under the fig tree. You knew He had a heart that beat for You. Each disciple was an ordinary man from a different walk of life that You strategically chose to follow You because they each could reach a specific people. You see each one of us in our quiet time and You can see right into each one of our hearts. Thank you.
In the precious name of Jesus we pray, Amen

THE MIRACLES

How did I miss those words?

Do whatever he tells you. ~John 2:5b, NIV.

Five words—spoken by His mother—the one who knew Him so well. It's not the words, but the actions which take place when the words are spoken, as a result of obedient hearts in the small things, because God cares about the small things, the hard things, and the big things.

**In God's perfect timing,
obedient hearts preceded the miracles.**

■ **Today's Scripture:**
Jesus turned water into wine at Cana.

His mother said to the servants, Do whatever he tells you. ~John 2:5b, NIV.

"Every man serves the good wine first, and when the people have drunk freely, then he serves the poorer wine; but you have kept the good wine until now." ~John 2:10

Jesus healed the leper in Gennesaret.

Jesus stretched out His hand and touched him, saying, "I am willing; be cleansed." And immediately his leprosy was cleansed. ~Matthew 8:3

When the disciples saw the storm in the Sea of Galilee, Jesus saw peace and stilled it.

He said to them, "Why are you afraid, you men of little faith?" Then He got up and rebuked the winds and the sea, and it became perfectly calm. ~Matthew 8:26

A woman could not stop bleeding, but she touched the hem of His cloak, and by faith, Jesus stopped the blood in Gennesaret.

…for she was saying to herself, "If I only touch His garment, I will get well." But Jesus turning and seeing her said, "Daughter, take courage; your faith has made you well." At once the woman was made well. ~Matthew 9:21-22

Jairus' saw his dying daughter, but Jesus saw life and healed her in Capernaum.

But when the crowd had been sent out, He entered and took her by the hand, and the girl got up. ~Matthew 9:25

day four

Jesus fed five thousand people in Bethsaida.

Ordering the people to sit down on the grass, He took the five loaves and the two fish, and looking up toward heaven, He blessed the food, and breaking the loaves He gave them to the disciples, and the disciples gave them to the crowds, and they all ate and were satisfied. They picked up what was left over of the broken pieces, twelve full baskets. ~Matthew 14:19-20

Jesus walked on the Sea of Galilee.

And in the fourth watch of the night He came to them, walking on the sea. ~Matthew 14:25

Jesus gave sight to the blind in Jericho.

They said to Him, "Lord, we want our eyes to be opened. Moved with compassion, Jesus touched their eyes; and immediately they regained their sight and followed Him." ~Matthew 20:33-34

Jesus performed many miracles.

Therefore many other signs Jesus also performed in the presence of the disciples, which are not written in this book; but these have been written so that you may believe that Jesus is the Christ, the Son of God; and that believing you may have life in His name. ~John 20:30-31

Miracles let us see, so we could believe, so we could let our encumbrances go and follow Him.

Therefore, since we have so great a cloud of witnesses surrounding us, let us also lay aside every encumbrance and the sin which so easily entangles us, and let us run with endurance the race that is set before us. ~Hebrews 12:1

■ **Today's Snapshot: The Miracles**
The miracles took place so that we could see, and by seeing we would believe, and by believing we would have life.

They followed Jesus and He performed miracles.

God gives us real examples to follow. Several great heroes of the Jewish faith belong in our faith-family tree—Abraham, Sarah, Isaac, Jacob, and Moses.

Today, God places people from our faith-family tree {moms, dads, sisters, brothers, friends, grandparents, teachers, coaches, youth workers, etc.} around us to help us, lead us, guide us, and encourage us. They are the witnesses who surround us as we run our race. They are our encouragers. They are our cheerleaders in this race called *life*.

To run our race today we *must* lay aside encumbrances and sins which hold us back. Encumbrances are burdens which we hold onto tightly. Sin is when we chose to not follow God.

If we are forgiven the moment we believe, why do we still carry around the boulders that keep us from running freely? He has told us to lay them at His feet, yet we keep picking them up again—we do not listen to Him.

We ask for miracles to occur in our lives, but we are still living the same way.

> *No one can serve two masters; for either he will hate the one and love the other,*
> *or he will be devoted to one and despise the other. ~Matthew 6:24*

God loved us so much that He sent His Son for us, so that we could be made new. His love changes our lives from being dead to being alive, so that we may walk in freedom—NOT so that we can go out and keep doing the same thing. God brought us into a relationship to change our hearts and to Set. Us. Free.

When we believe in Christ we become a new creation, which is a miracle in itself, and He gives us the ability to *do whatever He tells us.*

Therefore if anyone is in Christ, he is a new creature; the old things passed away; behold, new things have come. ~2nd Corinthians 5:17

■ **Family Discussion:**

- Has God told you to lay something aside? Get rid of something? Forgive someone? Trust Him in a situation?
- Has God performed a miracle for you that was bigger than you could have ever imagined?

■ **Closing Prayer:**

Heavenly Father,
We praise You for Your infinite presence in our lives—from the beginning of time to eternity. Thank You for the miracles. Please forgive us for our finite perspective on all matters. Please forgive us for making You weep. We pray that You would give us faith to trust You in all things because You can see the **big picture.** *May we continue to live our lives for You and bring You glory in all things.*
In the precious name of Jesus we pray, Amen

love

THE DECEPTIVE HEART

When my daughter began eating solid food, I fed her the same food I fed my son. I pureed the same fresh vegetables and served only the healthiest ingredients. While my son devoured everything I made, my daughter did not enjoy the flavor or the texture at all, and today they have completely different tastes. My son loves meat and potatoes and my daughter loves sugar!

We can try to parent our children in the same way, but each child is an individual person and he or she will receive our parenting differently. Ultimately, in the end, each one may choose to accept or walk away from our teachings.

And the world will try to convince them to walk away from the truth.

Lies deceive and distract from the truth of God's love and the reality of God's presence. Eternal separation from God began with the adversary who had a deceptive heart and told a lie. He wove his lies throughout history and ended up in the heart of Judas.

day five

■ Today's Scripture:

And He called the twelve together, and gave them power and authority over all the demons and to heal diseases and He sent them out to proclaim the kingdom of God and to perform healing. ~Luke 9:1-2

Now before the Feast of the Passover, Jesus knowing that His hour had come that He would depart out of this world to the Father, having loved His own who were in the world, He loved them to the end. During supper, the devil having already put into the heart of Judas Iscariot, the son of Simon, to betray Him, Jesus, knowing that the Father had given all things into His hands, and that He had come forth from God and was going back to God. ~John 13:1-3

When Jesus had spoken these words, He went forth with His disciples over the ravine of the Kidron, where there was a garden, in which He entered with His disciples. Now Judas also, who was betraying Him, knew the place, for Jesus had often met there with His disciples. Judas then, having received the Roman cohort and officers from the chief priests and the Pharisees, came there with lanterns and torches and weapons. So Jesus, knowing all the things that were coming upon Him, went forth and said to them, "Whom do you seek?"

They answered Him, "Jesus the Nazarene." He said to them, "I am He." And Judas also, who was betraying Him, was standing with them. So when He said to them, "I am He," they drew back and fell to the ground.

Therefore He again asked them, "Whom do you seek?" And they said, "Jesus the Nazarene." Jesus answered, "I told you that I am He; so if you seek Me, let these go their way," to fulfill the word which He spoke, "Of those whom You have given Me I lost not one." ~John 18:1-9

■ Today's Snapshot: The Deceptive Heart

Every single one of the twelve disciples witnessed the miracles that Jesus performed. Jesus gave each of them power and authority over all the demons to heal diseases, perform healings, and to proclaim the kingdom of God!

Judas walked with Jesus—side by side—for three years. Judas witnessed the miracles. He helped to pass out the bread. He was there when Jesus calmed the storm. While we read about what Jesus did, Judas experienced it all firsthand.

Each disciple sat underneath the same teaching from the Savior, but they didn't respond to Jesus the same way.

Judas's story is important. Sometimes we question ourselves when a child or a friend goes his or her own way against God. We question what we did wrong. Our hearts grieve over prodigal children.

We may all hear the same instruction, but each of us individually have control over our own choices. God knows our hearts' intentions and He sees the sins that ensnare us. Only God has the power to change someone's heart.

Regardless of all the goodness that we see and experience—just as Judas saw the best— we will not all choose to follow God. Some may still choose to turn and follow their own way.

■ **Family Discussion:**
- Have you ever made a selfish choice that did not honor God? Did you experience regret after you made it?
- What do you do when you see someone going down a path that may only lead to destruction?
- Do you think the other disciples knew what Judas was preparing to do?

■ **Closing Prayer:**
Heavenly Father,
We praise You for who You are and for Your unconditional love. You see us. You know us. You care for us. And You hope that we choose You in all things, but sometimes we don't. We're sorry for grieving You when we have gone our own ways. Thank You for never giving up on us. We are eternally grateful.
In the precious name of Jesus we pray, Amen

THE PERFECT LAMB

The shepherds whose flocks surrounded Bethlehem of Judea knew their lambs were chosen. These were the sacrificial lambs that were set apart to be used for the yearly Passover celebration—otherwise known as the Feast of Unleavened Bread when the Jewish people celebrate their deliverance out of the bonds of Egyptian slavery.

Joseph and Mary returned to Bethlehem in time for the census, but she was expecting a baby and there was no room in the inn. So, they found a warm place in a manger that had plenty of space for her to rest and deliver.

Mary swaddled her precious baby in muslin cloths just as the shepherds from that region must have wrapped each precious baby lamb—to keep them spotless and unblemished.

The life of the Perfect Lamb was flawless, and in the end, He became the ultimate, final sacrifice.

When God nailed Him to the cross,
His blood was shed for all of us.

love

By this will we have been sanctified through the offering of the body of Jesus Christ once for all. ~Hebrews 10:10

■ Today's Scripture:

Your lamb shall be an unblemished male a year old; you may take it from the sheep or from the goats. ~Exodus 12:5

Who has believed our message? And to whom has the arm of the LORD been revealed? For He grew up before Him like a tender shoot, and like a root out of parched ground; He has no stately form or majesty that we should look upon Him, nor appearance that we should be attracted to Him. He was despised and forsaken of men, a man of sorrows and acquainted with grief; and like one from whom men hide their face He was despised, and we did not esteem Him. ~Isaiah 53:1-3

But He was pierced through for our transgressions, He was crushed for our iniquities; The chastening for our well-being fell upon Him, and by His scourging we are healed. All of us like sheep have gone astray. Each of us has turned to his own way; but the LORD has caused the iniquity of us all to fall on Him. ~Isaiah 53:5-6

This is how God showed his love among us: He sent his one and only Son into the world that we might live through him. This is love: not that we loved God, but that he loved us and sent his Son as an atoning sacrifice for our sins. ~1 John 4:9-10, NIV

The next day John saw Jesus coming toward him and said, "Look, the Lamb of God, who takes away the sin of the world!" ~John 1:29, NIV

…how much more will the blood of Christ, who through the eternal Spirit offered Himself without blemish to God, cleanse your conscience from dead works to serve the living God? ~Hebrews 9:14

day six

Being found in appearance as a man, He humbled Himself by becoming obedient to the point of death, even death on a cross. ~Philippians 2:8

If you address as Father the One who impartially judges according to each one's work, conduct yourselves in fear during the time of your stay on earth; knowing that you were not redeemed with perishable things like silver or gold from your futile way of life inherited from your forefathers, but with precious blood, as of a lamb unblemished and spotless, the blood of Christ.
~1 Peter 1:17-19

For while we were still helpless, at the right time Christ died for the ungodly. For one will hardly die for a righteous man; though perhaps for the good man someone would dare even to die. ~Romans 5:6-7

There will be signs in the sun, moon and stars. On the earth, nations will be in anguish and perplexity at the roaring and tossing of the sea. People will faint from terror, apprehensive of what is coming on the world, for the heavenly bodies will be shaken. At that time they will see the Son of Man coming in a cloud with power and great glory. When these things begin to take place, stand up and lift up your heads, because your redemption is drawing near. ~Luke 21:25-28, NIV

They will wage war against the Lamb, but the Lamb will triumph over them because he is Lord of lords and King of kings--and with him will be his called, chosen and faithful followers. ~Revelation 17:14, NIV

And since we are his children, we are his heirs. In fact, together with Christ, we are heirs of God's glory. But if we are to share his glory, we must also share his suffering. ~Romans 8:17, NLT

■ Today's Snapshot: The Perfect Lamb

The Perfect Baby, born in the manger and wrapped in swaddling cloths, was the Perfect Lamb whom God sent to redeem His people from their sin once and for all.

This Perfect Baby was the last sacrificial lamb.
This Perfect Baby was the final redemption.

In the Old Testament, blood was shed as an offering for the forgiveness of sins because life is found in the blood. Instead of each one of us dying in our sin, Jesus became sin and died for us.

Pain—It is finished on the cross.
Suffering—It is finished on the cross.
Worry—It is finished on the cross.

All of your sins are finished on the cross.

We don't have to be afraid of today because we place our hope in the One who overcame.

Jesus overcame death, and one day so will we.

True victory is found in Him.

■ **Family Discussion:**
- Have you ever had to sacrifice anything in your life?
- How does it feel to know that Jesus became sin and died on the cross so that you could live forever?

■ **Closing Prayer:**
Heavenly Father,
We praise You for the Perfect Lamb who was born to be a sacrifice once and for all on the cross. We praise You for the greatest gift of Your Son who died for each one of us. We praise You for the blood that gives us life. We are eternally grateful. In the precious name of Jesus we pray, Amen

OUR LIVING HOPE

Upon arriving at Coligny, the public beach access on Hilton Head Island, my husband and I realized quickly that we were not the only ones with this bright idea. The people flocked in droves to the shoreline. Some wore jammies while some wore their Easter best, but all cheered, "He is Risen!" and responded, "He is Risen, indeed!" as the sun rose for the Easter-rise!

We need Him. We have needed Him to come from the very beginning.

After the fall, our separation from God caused the world to be dark. We needed the Light to come.

Over 2,000 years ago, Christ humbled Himself and took the punishment for the sin of the world upon Himself. He was beaten, shamed, and crucified for me.

On Christmas Eve we light the Christ candle.

If we did not have a world full of darkness, we would not need the Light.

We need the Light to see. So we were seeking joy, and we waited, and He worked.

Jesus always works in the waiting.

For the joy, He endured.
Jesus knew joy, saw joy, experienced joy, and became joy.

There is sadness, hate, and anger here today—and all we really want is joy.
On this journey called life, we all seek joy.

We look for joy in our families, best friends, and favorite activities. Joy is not found there. We look for joy in thrill-seeking adventures or relaxing beach escapes. Joy is not found there.

Where is joy when we need it most?

For the joy, Jesus endured the pain of becoming sin and the final sacrifice. Nothing is as difficult as the cross He endured, and nothing is as beautiful as the joy He experienced afterward.

■ **Today's Scripture:**
But God raised Him up again, putting an end to the agony of death since it was impossible for Him to be held in its power. ~Acts 2:24

Therefore, since we have so great a cloud of witnesses surrounding us, let us also lay aside every encumbrance and the sin which so easily entangles us, and let us run with endurance the race that is set before us, fixing our eyes on Jesus, the author and perfecter of faith, who for the joy set before Him endured the cross, despising the shame, and has sat down at the right hand of the throne of God. ~Hebrews 12:1-2

"He is not here; he has risen, just as he said. Come and see the place where he lay." ~Matthew 28:6, NIV

■ Today's Snapshot: Our Living Hope

He wasn't there. He was supposed to be there, but all they found was the napkin that covered His face. His body was gone.

Just as Jesus said He would do, Jesus conquered death and rose again! God keeps His promises. Jesus is alive!

■ Family Discussion:

• He wasn't there. Can you imagine if you were the one who arrived to see Jesus in His tomb and He was missing? What would you do? Who would you turn to?

■ Closing Prayer:

Heavenly Father,
We praise You for Your presence in our lives yesterday, today, and tomorrow. You have always been there for us. You take the sting of death away because You give us HOPE for eternal life. Thank You, Jesus. There are no words. We are grateful You have been there waiting for us—the entire time—to return to You. In the precious name of Jesus we pray, Amen

THE FAITH-FAMILY TREE

How far back can you trace your roots? Are you able to look back to see your parents' parents and where they descended from? Family-trees are fascinating because they show you exactly where you fit.

Every single heart longs for oneness . . . we long to fit in.

God preserved the imperishable seed of faith through the Hebrew people from Adam to Abraham to Moses to Esther to Obed to Jesse and to the heart of his son, King David. After 400 years of silence, a branch sprouted to continue the noble lineage.

■ **Today's Scripture: The Faith-Family Tree**
 For there is hope for a tree, When it is cut down, that it will sprout again, And its shoots will not fail. ~Job 14:7

Then a shoot will spring from the stem of Jesse, and a branch from his roots will bear fruit. ~Isaiah 11:1

And again, Isaiah says, "The Root of Jesse will spring up, one who will arise to rule over the nations; in him the Gentiles will hope." May the God of hope fill you with all joy and peace as you trust in him, so that you may overflow with hope by the power of the Holy Spirit. ~Romans 15:12-13, NIV

"I do not ask on behalf of these alone, but for those also who believe in Me through their word; that they may all be one; even as You, Father, are in Me and I in You, that they also may be in Us, so that the world may believe that You sent Me." ~John 17:20-21

If the part of the dough offered as firstfruits is holy, then the whole batch is holy; if the root is holy, so are the branches. If some of the branches have been broken off, and you, though a wild olive shoot, have been grafted in among the others and now share in the nourishing sap from the olive root, do not consider yourself to be superior to those other branches. If you do, consider this: You do not support the root, but the root supports you.
~Romans 11:16-18, NIV

And He is the radiance of His glory and the exact representation of His nature and upholds all things by the word of His power. When He had made purification of sins, He sat down at the right hand of the Majesty on high... ~Hebrews 1:3

For our citizenship is in heaven, from which also we eagerly wait for a Savior, the Lord Jesus Christ. ~Philippians 3:20

Christ was with God in the beginning (John 1:1).
He knew the beginning of the story, and He knows the end (Genesis 3:14-15).

He knew the promise.
He knew His purpose for descending to earth.
Through the womb of a woman, He came as fully man and fully God.
Jesus loved the same way God loved—completely and unconditionally.

Jesus knew no sin, yet He identified with our sin when He became sin for us on the cross. As a result, we identify with His righteousness.

> *He made Him who knew no sin to be sin on our behalf, so that we might become the righteousness of God in Him. ~2nd Corinthians 5:12*

**Here is the Good News—this is not the end of the story.
Death did not win!**

Jesus conquered death when He rose from the grave and returned to the Father—just as planned.

> *Where, O death, is your victory? Where, O death, is your sting?
> ~1 Corinthians 15:55, NIV*

Jesus returned to the Father.
Jesus returned to His roots.

> *So then, when the Lord Jesus had spoken to them, He was received up into heaven and sat down at the right hand of God. ~Mark 16:19*

From the beginning, our *Faith Roots* were firmly established in love.

Our *Faith Roots* reveal God's promise to each of us. When we say "yes" to Jesus—our Redeemer—our citizenship is rooted in Heaven forever. From that point forward we live with His power and his glory forever in us!

■ **Today's Snapshot: The Faith-Family Tree**

Jesus Christ's life in His earthly ministry reflected God's love.

God's love is patient. Jesus taught patience.
God's love is kind. Jesus taught kindness.
God's love is grace-filled. Jesus taught grace.
God's love is forgiving. Jesus taught forgiveness.

The Father's love radiated from within the heart of Christ. With every step He took, Jesus radiated the Father's love because Jesus is rooted in God's love.

When you believe, you are grafted into the faith-family tree and you fit perfectly! You belong here. You now have a new spiritual DNA, which makes you are a new creation!

Your *Faith Roots* go back to the beginning of time and you are rooted in radiance for eternity!

> *"I am Alpha and Omega, the beginning and the end, the first and the last."*
> *~Revelation 22:13*

■ Family Discussion:

- How does it feel to know you are "grafted in" forever to the faith-family tree that goes back to the beginning of time?

■ Closing Prayer:

Heavenly Father,
We praise You for sending Your Son to radiate Your glory on earth as it is in heaven. We praise You for giving Him the ability to lead us and teach us Your ways. We thank You for letting Him die for our sins and giving each one of us the gift of eternal life. We thank You for raising Him to life. He is our Living Hope. According to Your Word, we are raised with Him and we become citizens of heaven deeply rooted in His radiance.
In the precious name of Jesus we pray, Amen

IMMANUEL

Can you even imagine life with superpowers? Maybe we would be like Pixar's *The Incredibles?* Some days I need swiftness as I dash from home to school to home to church to sports and events throughout the week. Some days I need elasticity when I'm stretched so thin. Some days I just want to be invisible, because often I just need the craziness to go away. Every day, God knows exactly what I need, which is why He gives believers our very own superpower—a superpower so powerful that it was present with God at the beginning of time.

One morning I noticed the cool mist hovered over the lake in the Georgia Mountains. In my mind, I imagined this is what the Spirit of the Living God looked like as it hovered over the surface of the waters at the beginning of time. Its quiet presence—so beautiful, comforting, calming, and peaceful.

The Spirit of God, or the Breath of God, is *ruwach* in Hebrew. In the Old Testament, *ruwach* lived in the tabernacle {tent} and traveled with Moses through the wilderness and then *ruwach* lived, or dwelled, in the holy of holies {in the temple}.

Ezekiel paints the perfect picture in the valley of dry bones of what happens when God resurrects. God brings the dead to life. First He creates the body, then He breathes life into His creation, so that they may stand together as ONE powerful army.

When God breathed the breath of life into them, they stood together as one vast army. God breathed life into them because they were dead. Just like the dry bones, we are each dead in our sin (Romans 3:23).

advent

■ **Today's Scripture:**

> *In the beginning, God created the heavens and the earth. The earth was formless and void, and darkness was over the surface of the deep, and the Spirit of God was moving over the surface of the waters. ~Genesis 1:1-2*

> *So I prophesied as He commanded me, and the breath came into them, and they came to life and stood on their feet, an exceedingly great army. ~Ezekiel 37:10*

> *And they were all filled with the Holy Spirit and began to speak with other tongues, as the Spirit was giving them utterance. ~Acts 2:4*

> *But you will receive power when the Holy Spirit comes upon you, and you will be My witnesses in Jerusalem, and in all Judea and Samaria, and to the ends of the earth. ~Acts 1:8*

> *Go therefore and make disciples of all the nations, baptizing them in the name of the Father and the Son and the Holy Spirit, teaching them to observe all that I commanded you; and lo, I am with you always, even to the end of the age. ~Matthew 28:19-20*

> *"The virgin will conceive and give birth to a son, and they will call him Immanuel" (which means "God with us"). ~Matthew 1:23, NIV*

> *"Therefore the Lord Himself will give you a sign: Behold, a virgin will be with child and bear a son, and she will call His name Immanuel." ~Isaiah 7:14*

■ **Today's Snapshot: Immanuel**

But God sent His Son into this world in the flesh to teach us how to live with mercy and grace and to redeem us from our sin. Jesus, God's gift to us, offers forgiveness of our sins—yesterday, today, and tomorrow. When we understand the depth of His sacrificial love and turn to Him, He gives us the POWER of the Holy Spirit.

The Holy Spirit lives in us.
The Holy Spirit is your SUPERPOWER!

Being holy means we are set apart, yet joined together as He lives in us, to go therefore be my witnesses and make disciples.

His army grows.

We stand united in Him and that's a superpower.

God with us.
Us with God.
United as one.

Teach the Word. Observe the Word.
God is with us until the end of time!

■ **Family Discussion:**
- If you could have any superpower, what would you want it to be?
- God is with you always. Where do you need His power today?

■ **Closing Prayer:**
Heavenly Father,
*We praise You for the gift of the Holy Spirit who is a Superpower to all who believe. We praise You for the POWER of Your presence within each one of us who believes in You. You can see the **big picture**—while we can only see a snapshot of time—and You gave us the gift of the Holy Spirit to help us and bring us together as ONE for today. In the Spirit, we do not walk alone. In the Spirit, we move forward as ONE vast army, and together we will overcome, because You overcame!*
In the precious name of Jesus we pray, Amen

ADVENT

At eight days, right before His *bris*—the ritual of circumcision—they named Him Jesus. And after the thirty days of purification were finished, Joseph and Mary took Jesus to Jerusalem to present Him to the Lord. This Hebrew tradition of the redemption of the firstborn required them to take the sacrificial gift of two pigeons… *but in her arms lay one Perfect Lamb.*

Simeon saw him first. Full of the Holy Spirit, Simeon had been waiting a long time to see the Consolation of Israel. The Holy Spirit revealed to Simeon that he would not see death until he saw Jesus the Messiah. He was waiting for the One who would bring comfort and heavenly peace to the hurting world.

When Simeon saw the baby Jesus, Simeon instantly knew who He was and praised God.

The baby was to be a light to the Gentiles! Simeon blessed them, affirmed Jesus, and he shared wise words with them. He will be a sign, He will cause division, and people will speak against Him. Like a sword, your soul will be pierced. While God's redemption is free for all, it came at a great cost. Oh, how Simeon knew the deep pain that was to come! He encouraged Joseph and Mary to have hope because there will be victory in the end!

Each one of Anna's wrinkles told the story of her life. Anna, from the scattered tribe of Asher, never left the temple. She stayed there to fast and pray. One wise woman patiently waited to see the One who would be called the Redemption of Israel. Anna recognized Jesus immediately and gave thanks to God because her eyes had finally seen the Redemption of Israel.

Simeon and Anna both remembered that God keeps His promises!

■ Today's Scripture: Revelation

The Lord said to the serpent, "because you have done this, cursed are you more than all cattle, and more than every beast of the field; on your belly you will go, and dust you will eat all the days of your life; and I will put enmity between you and the woman and between your seed and her seed; He shall bruise you on the head, and you shall bruise him on the heel." ~Genesis 3:14-15

...and to wait for His Son from heaven, whom He raised from the dead, that is Jesus, who rescues us from the wrath to come. ~1 Thessalonians 1:10

"If I go and prepare a place for you, I will come again and receive you to Myself, that where I am, there you may be also." ~John 14:3

...and though you have not seen him, you love Him, and though you do not see Him now, but believe in Him, you greatly rejoice with joy inexpressible and full of glory, obtaining as the outcome of your faith the salvation of your souls. ~1 Peter 1:8-9

...for the Lamb in the center of the throne will be their shepherd, and will guide them to springs of the water of life; and God will wipe every tear from their eyes. ~Revelation 7:17

Let us rejoice and be glad and give the glory to Him, for the marriage of the Lamb has come and His bride has made herself ready. ~Revelation 19:7

"I, Jesus, have sent My angel to testify to you these things for the churches. I am the root and the descendant of David, the bright morning star." The Spirit and the bride say, "Come." And let the one who hears say, "Come." And let the one who is thirsty come; let the one who wishes take the water of life without cost. ~Revelations 22:16-17

Then I saw a new heaven and a new earth; for the first heaven and the first earth passed away, and there is no longer any sea. And I saw the holy city, new Jerusalem, coming down out of heaven from God, made ready as a bride adorned for her husband. And I heard a loud voice from the throne, saying, "Behold, the tabernacle of God is among men, and He will dwell among them, and they shall be His people, and God Himself will be among them, and He will wipe away every tear from their eyes; and there will no longer be any death; there will no longer be any mourning, or crying, or pain; the first things have passed away." And He who sits on the throne said, "Behold, I am making all things new." And He said, "Write, for these words are faithful and true." ~Revelation 21:1-5

■ Today's Snapshot: Advent

Simeon and Anna waited expectantly for the Messiah to arrive. Their wisdom, acquired from years spent in the Word, fasting, time in prayer, understanding God's promises, and their devotion to serving God's people in the temple, was admirable. There was no doubt that they knew Jesus would come to be the consolation of Israel and bring redemption for us all.

Jesus walked with us.

Jesus died for us.

By His wounds, we are healed.

Jesus reconciled us.

Jesus redeemed us.

Jesus makes our brokenness complete.

Once Jesus shed His blood as the final sacrifice, He rose to be with the Father, but the Father did not leave us alone. God sent the Comforter to live in us until the Savior comes again, this time to wipe away every tear and to finally make all things new.

Now Jesus lives in us by the power of the Holy Spirit and we are Simeon and Anna eagerly anticipating the Messiah's return.

With great expectation, we await His return.

When Jesus returns, the church will unite as the bride to meet the Groom in one final reunion. There will be a marriage of the Lamb and we will be welcomed to the eternal Kingdom of God.

■ **Family Discussion:**
- Jesus came to redeem us and bring us back to a whole, complete relationship with the Father. What part of your life has Jesus redeemed?
- Jesus gives us hope for today as we prepare for Him to return! Turn your eyes upon Jesus, and wait with hopeful expectation for the day of His return! What do you think life will be like when we are all together as one?

■ **Closing Prayer:**
Heavenly Father,
We praise You for Your presence yesterday, today, and tomorrow—from creation to the manger to the cross to the promise that one day You will return to wipe away our tears and make all things new. You alone are our Living Hope and in You alone, we place our trust. As Simeon and Anna waited with great expectation to see You, so do we! May we live every day with great anticipation of Your return! Please give us eyes to see Your presence today through the power of the Holy Spirit until You are physically present with us again.

While rooted in radiance we await Your precious return!
In the precious name of Jesus we pray, Amen

Introduction
1 *"Advent." Dictionary.com. https://www.dictionary.com/browse/advent.*

The Big Picture
2 *"C2000 Series on Genesis 1:1-8 by Chuck Smith." Blue Letter Bible.
   https://www.blueletterbible.org/Comm/smith_chuck/c2000_Gen/Gen_001a.cfm?a=1001.*

3 *"Genesis." Navigating the Bible II. http://bible.ort.org/books/torahd5.asp#C1.*

The Blessings
4 *https://www.blueletterbible.org*

The Tumultuous Twins
5 *https://www.livescience.com/16466-twins-multiple-birthsfascinating-facts.html*

The Perfect Baby
6 *Edersheim, Alfred. The Life and Times of Jesus the Messiah. Kindle ed. Packard Technologies, 2003.*

ABOUT THE AUTHOR

Mindy Lee Hopman is a Jewish believer, Bible teacher, author, and dynamic speaker with a Master of Arts degree in Religion from Liberty University with an emphasis in Christian Leadership. She also holds a Master of Arts degree in Education with an emphasis in Curriculum and Instruction from George Mason University.

Mindy's focus is on teaching believers how each person's individual faith story fits into the greatest story from the beginning to the end of time. Her grandfather was a great influence on her faith as a child, and even more as an adult when Mindy began to understand how her Christian faith directly connected to her Jewish roots.

Photographer Jon Aaron Hopman

Mindy's first book entitled ***Beautiful Legacy: Our Roots Run Deep*** uses personal narrative and Biblical application to trace the Jewish heritage of how one seed gives birth to the Christian faith-family tree. Mindy emphasizes the mystery of how, similar to the biblical olive tree, God grafts us into His faith-family tree in order for us to grow, thrive, and bear fruit. She helps readers recognize the origin of the Christian *Faith Roots* to pass the legacy on to future generations.

In her free time, Mindy delights in being with her family on the water boating or paddleboarding. She also enjoys walking her dogs (Jamaica & Champ), running in the early mornings, and taking sunrise/sunset pictures on the beautiful island where she lives.

*To share how God used **Faith Roots: An ADVENT Family Devotional** or to request a speaking engagement by Mindy, visit Mindy at her website Basking in His Light www.mindyhopman.com or email Mindy directly at mindyhopman@gmail.com*

ENCOURAGEMENT for the heart
NOURISHMENT for the soul

Mindy Lee Hopman's

BEAUTIFUL LEGACY:
OUR ROOTS RUN DEEP

It was a moment etched in time for author **Mindy Lee Hopman,** as she and her grandfather watched her children play. Her grandfather turned to her, and with tear-filled eyes whispered *naches*, Yiddish for unspeakable delight. That precious moment encouraged Hopman to wonder if she brought similar joy to her Heavenly Father. Thus was born the premise of her book, ***Beautiful Legacy: Our Roots Run Deep,*** in which Hopman traces the Jewish heritage to help readers understand how one seed gives birth to the ancient Hebrew-Christian faith-family tree.

Beautiful Legacy touched my soul. As a woman that was raised Catholic, with a Christian background and marrying into a Jewish family, I must say, this ties it all together. As I read through the book, I was taken to a deep level, and realized how deep our roots actually run. I felt sad when I finished the book, so I will read it again and again, as a practice. The message I got was, that we are all connected all the way back to the beginning. My faith is stronger and deeper than ever. Thank you Mindy, for sharing your story and bringing the message of GOD forward, again. ~ *Suzette Roth*

Beautiful Legacy is beautifully written and informative, penned by a teacher who lives her faith out loud. Mindy Lee Hopman helps guide you on your spiritual journey in the thought-provoking questions she presents in each chapter. She ties in Bible lessons to our current experiences of the world, and encourages us to apply those lessons to our personal stories. She breaks down the world view—how we see ourselves, how we live, etc.—and encourages us to turn that focus to God and to put Him at the center of our lives. Each chapter includes a spiritual discipline to help you grow in your faith as well as relevant scriptures, beautiful prayers and ample space for personal reflection.
~ *Kathy Odom*

Available now on Amazon